BYTES & BLISS

Bytes & Bliss

Achieving Inner Connection Amidst Digital Chaos

MARKIT

VR

MARKIT VENTURES

Contents

1

Prologue

If you've opened this book, it's because you're searching for something else, something that goes beyond the deafening noise of modern life. You are someone who moves with ease in the world of technology, but also someone who yearns for a deeper, more meaningful connection with yourself. Rest assured, this book, "Bytes & Bliss", has been written for you.

"Bytes & Bliss" is your map to navigate the technological maze that modern life proposes. It is not merely a book about personal development, but a journey towards self-discovery, internal development, and the realization of your life's purpose without feeling overwhelmed by technology. This journey is woven through emotional cinematic references and parallels with well-known world events, so you can see how your personal story intertwines with a broader narrative.

Do you remember that scene in "Terminator 2", where the advanced T-1000 relentlessly chases our heroes? That's a metaphor for how technology, when unchecked, can chase us down and impact our lives. What about that reflection in "Vanilla Sky" on the nature of reality and our perception of ourselves? That's the dilemma we face when balancing our digital and real identities.

This book will guide you through a journey of twelve chapters, each addressing essential aspects of our existence in the digital age. From exploring the interaction between man and technology to discovering our purpose and passion, this book will provide you with the tools to thrive in the digital world. It is not simply a manual. Far from being a series of prescribed steps to be followed to the letter, it is an invitation to reflection and introspection. Each chapter invites you to consider and reconsider your own experiences and perceptions. This is a book that expects you to question and probe yourself, to explore and experiment. After all, each of us is unique, and every path to self-discovery is personal.

In the end, this journey is not only about finding answers. It's more about learning to live the questions and discovering that true wisdom often lies in the most unexpected places.

As you go through Bytes & Bliss pages, you will feel empathy and understanding. We are all, in one way or another, navigating this digital sea, facing the same challenges.

In each chapter, I will challenge you to observe yourself, your relationships, your passions, your fears and your hopes. I will urge you to confront the distractions of modern life and focus on what truly matters. Through examples from popular movies and books, I will show you how others have navigated these challenges and have found their own path to a fulfilling life.

So I invite you to join me on this journey. No matter where you are on your path to self-discovery, there is room for you in "Bytes & Bliss". This book is a resource to help you navigate the eternal dance between man and technology, find your rhythm in the melody of life and discover how you can dance with grace and purpose. Together, we can learn to balance technology and our own humanity, so that we can live lives of Bytes and Bliss.

2

Acknowledgments

This book would not have been possible without the unwavering support, inspiration and help of many people. My most sincere gratitude to each of them, thank you for being there!

First and foremost, I want to dedicate this book to Vanina. It's impossible to express in words the gratitude I feel, our countless hours of shared conversations have been the essence and origin of this work. Her insightful observations about the world around us were crucial in shaping the themes and ideas we address in these pages. Her support, love and companionship have been a beacon for me on this journey.

To Marcela, whose talent and creativity have brought a new dimension to this book through her magnificent cover design. Her contribution has helped bring "Bytes & Bliss".

I also want to thank my family and friends, whose unconditional support has been fundamental in the realization of this project. Their encouragement and patience during this process have helped me overcome the toughest moments. Thanks to those who were there and thanks to those who are still here.

My deepest gratitude to Zacharias. His generous wisdom
and direction have been fundamental in this process. Without
his guidance, this book would not be what it is today.

Last but not least, my big thanks to Analia. Her meticulous
work in proofreading the English version of the book has
ensured that our vision can reach readers around the world
with accuracy.

To all of you, I offer my deepest thanks. Together, we have
created something that, with God's help, will inspire others to
seek their own inner connection amidst digital chaos. Each of
you has left an indelible mark on this book, and for that, I will
always be grateful.

Chapter 1

Man and Technology: The Eternal Dance

In the immortal words of Aldous Huxley, "Technological progress has merely provided us with more efficient means for going backward." These words from "Brave New World" author have echoed through the decades, a chilling reminder of a potential dystopia, a world where human connection and authenticity are casualties in the advance of technology.

Think back to the image of the Terminator, the epitome of an emotionless and unstoppable machine from the cult-classic movie "Terminator 2." This metallic beast, devoid of the warmth and empathy of human connection, exemplifies our fear of a world where technology replaces humanity. It's a world where the machines we created to serve us end up ruling us.

Pause for a second, and let's dig deep. Your journey isn't one of terror, but of awakening and transformation. Right now, the digital universe threatens to engulf you, every moment of your consciousness tethered to the tantalizing luster of screens. Emails, notifications, updates - they're relentless, your ever-present chains. You're navigating a strange new world of your own creation, a place where reality and the digital blur together.

There may come a day when you catch your reflection in the screen, estranged from the pulsating life around you. Your loved ones morph into mere pixels, their radiant smiles turned into frozen, emotionless emojis. It's a harsh truth, a thunderclap of reality that shakes you to your very core. You're stuck in your personal "Terminator 2" nightmare, a universe where machines commandeer your life.

However, this is the moment to rewrite the story, to reshape your bond with technology. You're not meant to be the passive prey of your gadgets. You must aspire to be the Sarah Connor of your own existence, a lighthouse of humanity in a realm teetering on the precipice of technological rule. It's time to venture out on a quest to recapture your human bond, your authenticity and essence.

It's not going to be an effortless quest. It's a dance, an eternal ballet between humanity and technology, full of missteps and faltering. Yet with each step, you'll learn to traverse this complex dance floor, to discover a rhythm that enables you to utilize technology without getting lost in its encompassing grip.

This adventure will propel you into the swift progression of 21st-century technology, a global phenomenon that has irreversibly transformed the panorama of human existence. It's a formidable reality, one that could render us feeling powerless, adrift in the ceaseless tidal wave of progress.

But I am here to say: it doesn't have to be like this. You possess the power to alter your story, to master this everlasting dance with technology. It's not about renouncing technology, but about finding a balance, a rhythm that lets you exploit its advantages without sacrificing your essence.

In this chapter, we will explore the history of man and technology, understand its impact on modern life, and delve into the challenges and opportunities it presents. Most importantly, we will discover how to balance technology use and human connection, a delicate dance that can lead us to a future where bytes and bliss coexist harmoniously.

Are you ready to join this dance? Are you ready to claim back your humanity in this brave new world? It's time to rise, not as a passive observer but as an active participant, as the master of your destiny. It's time to dance baby! Look at Technology's eyes and ask her to dance.

Section 1: The History of Man and Technology

Imagine standing on the precipice of a new age, peering into the vast expanse of the unknown, the future, where technology is the dance partner leading us into tomorrow. Like the characters in Aldous Huxley's "Brave New World," we're caught in the flux of unprecedented change. We're the architects of a world where machines aren't just tools; they are an inseparable part of our existence, guiding our steps in this eternal dance of man and technology.

Remember John Connor from "Terminator 2," a beacon of humanity in a dystopian future where machines threaten to seize control? He was a symbol of resistance, a testament to the indomitable human spirit that refuses to be overshadowed by the cold, emotionless precision of artificial intelligence. But, unlike the future foretold in the movie, our reality is not as grim. We are not at war with machines; instead, we are engaged in a symbiotic relationship, a pirouette, in which every move we make influences the following one.

Our technology journey is like an epic tale, spanning across eras, each chapter marked by inventions that revolutionized human existence. From the invention of the wheel, which set us on the road to progress, to the development of the printing press, which democratized knowledge, technology has been our ally, a silent partner that has fueled our evolution.

Just as in Huxley's "Brave New World," we've harnessed the power of technology to shape society and human behavior. We've created machines that think, learn, and even dream, a reality that not too long ago belonged solely to the realm of science fiction. We've built a digital landscape so expansive that it rivals our physical reality, a brave new world where boundaries are blurred, and possibilities are endless.

However, with great power comes great responsibility. Technology, in all its glory, is a double-edged sword. It can serve as a beacon of progress, illuminating our path towards a brighter future, or it can cast a long, ominous shadow that threatens to eclipse our humanity, much like the rogue AI in "Terminator 2."

We stand at a crossroads, just as John Connor, with the future of humanity resting on our shoulders. Our choices will determine whether we dance in harmony with technology or step on each other's toes, creating a discord that disrupts the melody of progress.

Nevertheless, unlike the dystopian future depicted in "Terminator 2," we have the power to shape our destiny. We are not helpless spectators, waiting for an AI apocalypse. Instead, we are active participants in this dance, capable of steering our partner, technology, towards a future where it enhances our lives rather than overpowering them.

Let this sink in: We are the choreographers of our dance with technology. We decide the rhythm, the pace, and the direction of this dance. We have the power to ensure that technology serves us, aids us, and uplifts us, rather than controlling or diminishing us. And how do we do that?

By becoming conscious dancers. By understanding our history with technology, recognizing the impact it has on our lives, and foreseeing the challenges and opportunities it presents. By learning the steps that lead to harmony and balance, and by taking bold strides towards a future where technology and humanity exist in a mutually beneficial partnership.

So, I urge you, step onto the dance floor with conviction and optimism. Embrace technology as a partner, not an adversary. Let's dance this eternal dance together, with grace, courage, and an unwavering belief in our ability to shape our destiny.

Remember, you are not alone in this dance. Just as John Connor had Sarah and The Terminator by his side, you too are surrounded by a community of fellow dancers, all navigating this brave new world together. We're all learning, adapting, and growing in this dynamic dance of life, with technology as our dance partner.

As we move into the next part of this chapter, we'll delve deeper into the impact of technology on our modern life. We will discuss how it has revolutionized communication, transformed how we work, learn, and play, and even changed the very fabric of our social relationships. We'll also explore the challenges this rapid technological advancement presents, such as privacy concerns, digital addiction, and the fear of becoming too dependent on our digital companions.

And, most importantly, we'll discuss the opportunities that this brave new world offers. We'll explore how technology can be used to enhance our lives, empower us, and even help us grow as individuals. We'll look at the ways technology can aid in self-discovery, foster creativity, and even help us connect with others on a deeper level.

But remember, this journey is not merely about understanding technology; it's about understanding ourselves in relation to technology. It's about finding balance, cultivating a healthy relationship with our digital counterparts, and learning to dance in harmony with them. It's about making sure that we lead this dance, that we guide technology to serve our needs and aspirations, and not the other way around.

So, as we continue this journey, I encourage you to approach it with an open mind and a willingness to learn. Remember, this is not just a dance with technology; it's a dance with ourselves. It's about understanding who we are, what we are worth and how we can use technology to become the best versions of ourselves.

So, let's step onto the dance floor with confidence and anticipation. Let's embrace the music, feel the rhythm and enjoy the dance. Remember, it's not about perfecting the steps; it's about enjoying the journey. As we move forward, let's remember what John Connor in Terminator 2 said: "The future's not set. There's no fate but what we make for ourselves." Let's make our future a harmonious dance with technology.

Section 2: The Impact of Technology on Modern Life

The world we live in is a far cry from the one depicted in Aldous Huxley's "Brave New World". Yet, some of the themes resonate with our present reality. Technology has become an integral part of our daily lives, influencing how we work, learn, communicate, and even how we perceive ourselves. This influence isn't inherently negative, nevertheless, as all powerful tools, it comes with its share of challenges.

Just as in "Brave New World", where citizens are conditioned from birth to conform to societal norms and expectations, we too, in this digital era, are subtly guided by the algorithms that boost our social media feeds, search engines, and even our shopping habits. We're constantly bombarded with notifications, messages, and updates, which can lead to a sense of being overwhelmed and disconnected from our own thoughts and feelings.

Moreover, these algorithms create a sort of digital echo chamber, where we're more likely to encounter information that aligns with our existing beliefs and interests, thus limiting our exposure to diverse perspectives and ideas. This can lead to a narrow view of the world, similar to the conditioned citizens of Huxley's dystopian society.

However, it's not all dystopian gloom. Just as the Terminator was reprogrammed in "Terminator 2" to protect and guide, technology also can be guided to serve us positively. It has undeniably made our lives easier and more convenient. We can connect with people across the globe, access vast amounts of information at the click of a button, and automate mundane tasks, freeing up time for more meaningful pursuits.

But how do we make sure that we, like John Connor, keep in control of our technological creations? How do we harness the benefits of technology while mitigating the challenges it presents?

The key lies in balance and mindful use of technology. Like any tool, technology itself is neutral; it's how we use it that determines its impact on our lives. By becoming more mindful and intentional in our use of technology, we can avoid the pitfalls of digital overload and instead use it as a tool for personal growth and development.

In the following sections, we are going to explore practical strategies for achieving this balance, from setting boundaries with our devices, to cultivating digital wellness habits, and using technology as a tool for self-discovery and personal growth.

Remember, technology is a part of our modern lives, but it doesn't have to dictate our lives. Just as John Connor controlled the Terminator, we too have the power to control our relationship with technology. We can choose to dance to the rhythm of our own music, creating a dance that is uniquely ours. It's a dance of balance, a dance of mindfulness and, most importantly, a dance of personal growth and self-discovery. Let's lead this dance and steer our relationship with technology towards a path of Bytes and Bliss.

Section 3: The Challenges and Opportunities Presented by Technology

As you set forth on your own expedition of technological self-exploration, you'll frequently find yourself reflecting on the core theme of Huxley's "Brave New World" – the tug-of-war between individuality and social uniformity. Just like the figures within the novel's pages, you too are ensnared in a vortex of societal demands, pressures, and the formidable sway of technology.

We're living in an age where our devices and algorithms often know more about us than we know about ourselves. They predict our needs, suggest our next purchases, and even influence our opinions. But, while this level of personalization can be incredibly convenient, it also poses a challenge to our self-perception and individuality.

We are continuously nudged to conform to certain behaviors, to crave the validation of likes and shares, and to compare ourselves with others. It's a bit like the characters in

"Brave New World" who are conditioned to conform and to avoid individuality and solitude at all costs.

This constant exposure to an idealized version of reality can lead to feelings of inadequacy and a distorted self-image. It can be challenging to remember that what we see online is often a highlighted reel, not the full story. The struggle to distinguish between our real selves and our digital personas can create a disconnection within us.

Yet, just as the Terminator in "Terminator 2" was re-programmed to serve a higher purpose, we too can repurpose our technology use. We can choose to see the challenges as opportunities for growth and transformation.

We can use technology as a tool for self-expression and creativity, to learn and grow and to connect meaningfully with others. By harnessing the power of technology mindfully, we can break free from the constraints of digital conformity and rediscover our authentic selves.

Imagine using technology to foster genuine connections, to learn new skills, to explore different perspectives and ideas. Imagine using it as a tool to understand ourselves better, to reflect on our values and goals, and to express our individuality.

In the next sections, we'll delve deeper into the impact of technology on our identities and relationships. We'll explore strategies for cultivating authenticity in a digital world and for balancing our technology use with our human needs and aspirations.

Just as John Connor guided the Terminator towards a higher purpose, we too can guide our technology use towards personal growth and self-discovery. We can create a digital world that reflects our true selves, nurturing our personal and spiritual growth. The choice is ours. Let's seize this opportunity to redefine our relationship with technology and to create a dance that celebrates our individuality and humanity.

Section 4: Balancing Technology Use and Human Connection

In the grand dance between man and technology, there comes a point where we must pause to consider the rhythm and direction of our movements. Just as a dancers must find balance and harmony in their steps, we must find balance and harmony in our relationship with technology.

In this age of connectivity, our devices often seem like extensions of ourselves. They accompany us throughout our day, from the moment we wake up until we fall asleep. Yet, as well as our physical bodies need rest, our digital selves also need periods of disconnection and solitude.

We must learn to create spaces in our lives that are free from digital distractions, spaces where we can connect with ourselves and with others on a deeper, more meaningful level. Exactly like in the movie "Terminator 2," where Sarah Connor finds solace and strength in moments of solitude, we too can find inner peace and clarity in moments of digital disconnection.

Remember the scene in the movie where Sarah carves "No Fate" into a table? She realizes that they have the power to shape their own destiny. Just like her, we too have the power to shape our digital destiny. We can choose when to engage with technology and when to disengage. We can choose to use it as a tool for connection and growth, rather than letting it rule our lives.

In our dance with technology, we must remember that we are the choreographers. We set the rhythm and pace. We decide when to step forward and when to step back. We decide when to engage and when to disconnect.

In the next chapter, we'll explore the true meaning of self-discovery in the digital age. We'll delve deeper into the struggle between our virtual and real selves and examine the impact of technology on our self-perception.

Just as the characters in "Brave New World" and "Terminator 2" found their own paths amidst societal pressures and technological advancements, we also can find our unique paths in this digital world. We can learn to balance our technology use with our human needs, to cultivate authenticity, and to foster genuine human connections.

In the grand dance between man and technology, we must remember that it's our dance. We set the rhythm, lead the steps and shape the direction. Let's seize this opportunity to create a dance that reflects our true selves, our values and our aspirations.

Conclusion and Action Steps

As we conclude this exploration of the entwined dance between man and technology, we find ourselves standing at a crossroads. The rapid evolution of technology in the 21st century, akin to the dystopian futures imagined in "Brave New World" and "Terminator 2," underscores the urgency of our decision. Are we going to let our devices dictate our lives, or are we going to reclaim our autonomy, crafting a future that aligns with our deepest truths?

This chapter examined the complex relationship we have with technology, but it was not to evoke fear or despair. On the contrary, it is a call to action, an invitation to seek balance and harmony, just as a dancer would on the dance floor.

Now, it's time for you to lead your dance with technology. To get you on this journey, here are five action steps to start with:

Perform a Digital Audit: Spend a week consciously observing your use of technology. Note down the time spent on various devices and what you do during that time. This will provide you with a clear picture of your current habits. Also, cultivate awareness and pay attention to how and when you use technology. Notice how it impacts your emotions, your relationships, and your sense of self.

Set Clear Boundaries: Decide on specific times for technology use and stick to them. For example, you could decide not to use your phone for an hour after waking up and an hour before going to bed, or to have a screen-free room in your house. Create tech-free zones and times in your day.

Cultivate Offline Interests: Engage in activities that don't involve technology. This could be reading a physical book, gardening, painting, doing outdoor sports, or simply spending time in nature. Practice digital detox regularly to disconnect from the virtual world and reconnect with your inner self.

Practice Mindful Use of Technology: Whenever you use your devices, do so with intention. Avoid mindless scrolling and aim to use technology for a specific purpose. Always ask yourself, Is this aligned with whom I want to become? Be mindful of your online activities. Use technology as a tool for growth and connection, not a source of distraction or escape.

Create Spaces for Human Connection: Dedicate specific times for interacting with loved ones, without the interference of technology. This could be during meals, or setting aside a technology-free evening every week. Invest time in real-world relationships. Use technology to facilitate, not replace, genuine human interaction.

The dance between man and technology is eternal, but its rhythm, pace, and direction are yours to determine. As we embark on this journey together, remember the importance of every small step towards balance and mindfulness. You have the power, just like Sarah Connor did, to shape your own digital destiny. It's time to embrace the dance with technology, not with fear or resistance, but with understanding, empathy, and a clear vision of the future.

This is your journey and it begins now. It's time to master the art of balancing bytes and bliss.

Chapter 2

Self-Discovery in
the Digital Age

In the world created in the movie ¨Vanilla Sky¨, the protagonist David Aames found himself living an artificial life, a dreamlike state, where reality and illusion became indistinguishable. This narrative, though set in a surreal cinematic universe, resonates with our own reality in an eerily profound way. The advent of social media platforms, the rise of digital personas, the creation of online identities - these world events have ushered us into an era where we, too, often struggle to distinguish the real from the virtual.

Our screens have become mirrors, reflecting back to us not what we are, but what we aspire to be, or what others expect us to be. The filters and emojis, likes and shares, have crafted a Vanilla Sky for each of us, a surreal dreamscape that often veils our authentic selves. This chapter is about peeling back that veil. It's about navigating the maze of the digital age and finding oneself in the process.

We promise to delve deep into the heart of this modern struggle, exploring the intricate dance between our digital and real-world identities. We will go together through the following sections:

Virtual Me Vs Real Self: Who am I? - Here, we'll dissect the contrast between our digital personas and our true selves, exploring the potential dissonance between the two.

Digital Identity Vs Real-World Identity - This section will shed light on how our online and offline identities may differ and what this disparity means for our self-perception and personal development.

Impact of Technology on Self-Perception - We will investigate how our digital presence influences our view of ourselves and our place in the world.

Cultivating Authenticity in a Digital World - Lastly, we will offer strategies for nurturing genuineness and personal growth amidst the noise and distractions of our hyperconnected lives.

With each section, you'll gain new insights, acquire practical tools, and hopefully, move closer to a more authentic, self-aware version of yourself, one who can navigate the Vanilla Sky of the digital world without losing sight of their true purpose.

Section 1: Virtual Me Vs Real Self: Who am I?

Just as David Aames in Vanilla Sky grappled with the enigma of his existence, we too are facing a similar challenge in the digital age. The lines between our virtual selves and our real selves are becoming increasingly blurred.

Your digital persona, the one that exists in social media, the one that garners likes, shares and comments, is an entity of its own. It's often an idealized version of you, curated with the most exciting and attractive parts of your life. It's you, but through a filter—literally and figuratively. The perfect selfie after twenty attempts, the awe-inspiring vacation shot taken after hours of searching for the perfect angle, the witty comment crafted after careful thought and multiple revisions. These curated snapshots often depict a life that is more exciting, more flawless than our real, lived experience.

And then, there's the real you. The one who wakes up with messy hair, occasionally trips over their own feet and sometimes feels lost or inadequate. This is the you who laughs, cries, loves, and feels. This you isn't always picture-perfect, but it's genuine, authentic and beautiful in its own unique way.

In the digital age, it's easy to get so caught up in curating our virtual selves that we start to lose touch with our real selves. We start to measure our worth based on the number of likes or followers we have, we start to compare our behind-the-scenes with others' highlight reels. This can lead to feelings of inadequacy, self-doubt, and even identity confusion.

So, who are you, really? Are you the meticulously curated persona presented online, or are you the unfiltered, imperfectly perfect human experiencing life in all its ups and downs? Recognizing the dissonance between our virtual selves and our real selves is the first step towards self-discovery in the digital age.

Section 2: Digital Identity Vs Real-World Identity

We've digged into the chasm between our digital persona and our real self. Now, let's delve deeper into the dichotomy between our digital identity and real-world identity. Just like David Aames in Vanilla Sky, we may often find ourselves caught between the allure of a fabricated reality and the grounding truth of our actual existence.

Our digital identities, like characters in a grand digital play, are built upon selective self-presentation. We choose what to post, what to say, who to interact with and, in doing so, we craft a narrative about who we are—or rather, who we want others to believe we are. This digital identity can become a mask, a façade that offers both a sense of control and a shield from real-world judgment.

Our real-world identities, however, are far more nuanced. They are shaped by our actions, ` interactions, triumphs and failures. They encompass not only our public personas but also private thoughts, vulnerabilities and doubts. Unlike our digital identities, our real-world identities cannot be edited or filtered; they are raw and real.

The disparity between our digital and real-world identities can lead to a jarring disconnection, a dissonance that, if left unaddressed, can cause emotional distress. We might feel pressured to live up to the perfection of our online selves, leading to feelings of inadequacy when our real lives don't measure up. Conversely, we might feel alienated and dis-connected, living a life online that doesn't truly reflect who we are.

This divergence isn't necessarily harmful. Our digital identity can serve as a creative outlet, a platform for self-expression, a means to connect with like-minded individuals worldwide. The key lies in recognizing and managing this dichotomy, ensuring that our digital identities serve us rather than define us.

Section 3: The Impact of Technology on Self-Perception

The realm of the digital has become an omnipresent force in our lives, shaping not just our interaction with the world but also our perception of ourselves. Like the protagonist in

Vanilla Sky, we may find ourselves lost in the maze of our own creation, struggling to discern our true selves amidst the noise of the virtual world.

The impact of technology on self-perception is multi-layered. On one hand, it can bolster self-esteem and foster a sense of belonging. The ability to connect, share, and receive feedback can create an environment of validation and camaraderie. It provides a platform to express our thoughts, ideas, and creativity, often contributing to a positive sense of self.

On the other hand, this constant exposure to the digital sphere can lead to a skewed sense of self. We are continuously bombarded with curated highlights of other people's lives, leading us to compare and often feel inadequate. Our self-esteem may start hinging on the number of likes, comments, or followers we receive, shifting our self-worth from an intrinsic to an extrinsic measure.

Moreover, the digital world encourages us to adopt a performance mindset. We are always 'on,' always in the public eye, always under pressure to portray an idealized version of ourselves. This performance can eventually lead to a disconnection from our authentic selves, as we start identifying more with the character we play online.

This is not to paint a bleak picture of technology and its impacts, but rather to illuminate the potential challenges that come with it. Awareness is the first step towards change. By understanding how technology influences our self-perception, we can start making mindful choices that serve our well-being and foster a healthier relationship with our digital selves.

Section 4: Cultivating Authenticity in a Digital World

In a world where our digital identities often overshadow our real-world selves, cultivating authenticity can seem like a daunting task. However, just like David Aames in Vanilla Sky finally found a way to distinguish his dreams from reality, we can learn to foster authenticity in our digital lives too.

Authenticity starts with self-awareness, with understanding who we truly are beyond the curated narratives of our digital personas. It's about recognizing our values, our passions, our strengths, and our weaknesses, and living in alignment with them. It's about embracing our imperfections and vulnerabilities, understanding that they make us human.

In the digital sphere, authenticity translates into showing up as our true selves. This doesn't mean oversharing or putting every aspect of our lives on display. Rather, it's about aligning our digital identities with our real-world selves. It's about being honest, being genuine, and being real.

One way to cultivate authenticity online is to use social media mindfully. Before posting, ask yourself: Does this reflect who I truly am? Am I sharing this to seek validation or because it genuinely resonates with me? Over time, these mindful checks can help you build a digital identity that aligns with your authentic self.

Another strategy is to embrace vulnerability. The digital world often pushes us to portray an image of perfection. Breaking away from this norm and sharing our struggles and failures can not only foster authenticity but also build deeper connections with others.

Remember, cultivating authenticity is a journey, not a destination. It's about progress, not perfection. As we continue to navigate the digital landscape, let's strive to bring more of our authentic selves into the virtual world.

Conclusion and Action Steps

In *Vanilla Sky*, David Aames eventually managed to separate the illusions of his dream world from the reality of his existence. Our journey in the digital age echoes his quest. As we navigate the labyrinth of our online personas and the reality of our offline selves, we are challenged to discern the line between the two and cultivate authenticity.

The digital age brings both opportunities and challenges. It provides a platform for self-expression and connection, but it can also create a dissonance between our online personas and our authentic selves. But remember, you are not the number of likes on your latest post or the follower count on your profile. You are a complex, multifaceted individual with a unique story to tell.

The journey to self-discovery and authenticity in the digital age is a journey of awareness, understanding and mindful action. Here are five action steps to guide you on this path:

Mindful posting: Before you post, pause and reflect. Ask yourself: Is this a true reflection of me? Am I sharing this for validation or because it resonates with me?

Digital detox: Disconnect from your devices regularly. Use this time to reconnect with yourself, your loved ones and the world around you.

Authentic interactions: Strive to be genuine in your online interactions. Engage in conversations that align with your interests and values.

Comparison check: If you find yourself comparing your life to others' highlight reels, remind yourself that social media isn't a complete picture of anyone's life.

Embrace imperfection: It's okay not to be perfect. Share your struggles, failures and your ride. Authenticity fosters connection.

Embarking on this journey may seem daunting, but remember, each step brings you closer to your authentic self. Just as David Aames found his way through his illusory world, you too can navigate the digital age with authenticity and grace.

Chapter 3

Mindset Matters: Finding Internal Connection

As we venture deeper into the core of our digital age, it's essential to recognize the profound insights shared by Eckhart Tolle in his transformative work "The Power of Now: A Guide to Spiritual Enlightenment". Tolle teaches us to treasure the present moment, to separate our true selves from our thoughts, and to embrace the reality that we are not the fleeting digital profiles we've constructed, but deeply spiritual beings yearning for connection and growth.

Parallel to Tolle's timeless wisdom, we're witnessing a globally impactful event that resonates with the essence of this chapter – the increasing recognition of technology's effect on our mental health and well-being. The omnipresence of smartphones and social media, once hailed as the pinnacle of connectivity, has begun to cast long, disquieting shadows on our inner peace. We're more "connected" than ever, yet we feel isolated, anxious, and disconnected from our true selves. This paradox of modern connectedness under-scores the urgency of our quest for internal connection.

In this chapter, we promise to explore the profound relationship between your mindset and your ability to develop deep internal connections. We will delve into the paradox of modern connectedness, the consequences of internal dis-connection, the power of reconnecting with nature and our inner selves, and strategies for cultivating a balanced mindset in a digital world.

Section 1: The Paradox of Modern Connectedness

Our journey begins with an exploration of the paradox of modern connectedness. How is it that in a hyper-connected world by technology, we feel increasingly disconnected from our true selves and the people around us? We are in constant contact, but feel more alone than ever. Through this explora-tion, we aim to unravel the complex web of digital interaction and its influence on our internal well-being.

Section 2: The Consequences of Internal Disconnection

As we progress, we are going to delve into the conse-quences of internal disconnection. What happens when we lose touch with our inner selves? How does this affect our relationships, purpose and our overall well-being? Under-standing these consequences is the first step in our journey towards reconnection.

Section 3: Reconnecting with Nature and Our Inner Selves

Next, we are going to explore the profound power of re-connecting with nature and our inner selves. We'll look into practical strategies and exercises that will guide you in rediscovering your internal compass, understanding your true desires and obtaining a deeper connection with the world around you.

Section 4: Cultivating a Balanced Mindset in a Digital World

Finally, we will guide you in cultivating a balanced mindset in a digital world. We are going to share tools and strategies to help you maintain a strong inner connection even amidst the chaos and distraction of digital living. You are gonna learn to balance your use of technology with your need for self-reflection, purpose and inner peace.

In the following sections, we are embarking on a journey of self-discovery, where you will learn to silence the noise of modern living, embrace the power of mindfulness, and re-claim your authentic self. This is not a journey of escape but rather a journey of balance, a journey to a place where bytes and bliss coexist.

Section 1: The Paradox of Modern Connectedness

In the age of information, our lives are filled with a relent-less stream of digital interactions. From the moment we wake up to the moment we fall asleep, our screens bombard us with emails, notifications, messages, likes and shares. This omni-present technology promises us a world of connectivity, where distances are bridged and communication is instan-taneous. But beneath the glossy veneer of this digital utopia, a troubling paradox emerges.

Although we're connected more than ever in the physical sense, we're often left feeling emotionally and spiritually dis-connected. Our digital connections, as vast and complex as they may be, can't replicate the depth and richness of face-to-face human interaction. We've traded meaningful conversa-tions for text messages, genuine laughter for emojis and heartfelt expressions of love for quick taps on the 'like' button. In the process, we've created a digital facsimile of connection, leaving many of us feeling strangely alone amidst the crowd.

Moreover, our digital devices have turned us into consumers of other people's lives, often leaving us feeling inadequate or unfulfilled. As we scroll through seemingly perfect snapshots of other people's lives, we can't help but compare them to our own. This comparison breeds discontent, and the more we engage in it, the more disconnected we become from our own reality, our own joys and achievements.

Our digital lives also leave little room for introspection and self-discovery. We're so absorbed in the external world of likes, shares and followers that we often neglect the internal world of thoughts, emotions, and desires. This obsession with the external can lead us to feel disconnected from our inner selves, leaving us feeling lost and purposeless in a world that's more connected than ever.

And, finally our constant digital connectivity leaves us with little time for solitude – a state of being that's essential for self-reflection, creativity and internal connection. In the words of philosopher Blaise Pascal, "All of humanity's problems stem from man's inability to sit quietly in a room alone." As we fill every idle moment with screen time, we rob ourselves of the chance to connect with our thoughts, our feelings, and our inner selves.

The paradox of modern connectedness is a complex and multifaceted problem. However, by acknowledging its existence and understanding its consequences, we take the first step toward overcoming it. In the next section, we will delve deeper into the effects of internal disconnection and explore how it impacts our lives.

Section 2: The Consequences of Internal Disconnection

Internal disconnection, the state of being out of touch with our true selves, carries profound consequences. It casts a shadow over our lives, obscuring our path and making every step feel heavier than it should. It's a silent epidemic of the digital age, largely unseen but keenly felt, touching every aspect of our lives.

One of the most significant consequences of internal disconnection is a pervasive sense of loneliness. Even surrounded by a sea of digital interactions, we may feel isolated and misunderstood. Without a firm grounding in our own identity, we can struggle to form deep, meaningful relationships, leading to a profound sense of emotional isolation.

Furthermore, internal disconnection can manifest as a sense of meaninglessness or purposelessness. As we lose touch with our inner selves, we lose sight of our goals, values and passions. Life can start to feel like a series of disconnected events, devoid of purpose or direction. We may feel as if we're merely existing rather than truly living.

A disconnection from our inner selves also impacts on our ability to make authentic, fulfilling decisions. Guided by external influences, rather than our inner compass, we can find ourselves making choices that don't align with our true desires. This disconnection between our actions and our authentic selves can lead to regret, dissatisfaction and a nagging sense of unfulfilled potential.

Perhaps, the most pervasive consequence of internal disconnection, however, is its impact on our mental health. Research increasingly suggests that a lack of inner connection can contribute to anxiety, depression and chronic stress. Without an internal connection, we're ill-equipped to manage our emotions, leading to increased vulnerability to mental health issues.

The consequences of internal disconnection can be severe, but there's hope. The solution lies not in rejecting our digital lives, but in finding a balance. By integrating our digital experiences with our need for internal connection, we can create a more fulfilling, purpose-driven life.

In the next section, we are exploring the transformative power of reconnecting with nature and our inner selves, providing you with practical strategies to bridge the gap between your digital and spiritual life.

Section 3: Reconnecting with Nature and Our Inner Selves

In a world that's always buzzing, blinking and insisting on our attention, it's easy to lose touch with our inner selves. Reconnecting with our inner world, however, is not a luxury but a necessity. One of the most effective ways to achieve this is through the therapeutic embrace of nature.

Nature, with its unhurried rhythm and serene beauty, stands in stark contrast to our fast-paced digital lives. It encourages introspection, presence and mindfulness – all essential elements of internal connection. When we immerse ourselves in nature, we're able to step away from the digital whirlwind and engage deeply with our thoughts and emotions. We experience the power of 'now', the very concept that Eckhart Tolle defends in his work. This practice of being fully present allows us to tune into our inner dialogue, fostering a deeper understanding of ourselves.

Exercises such as mindful walks or meditative stargazing can be particularly effective in fostering this connection. By focusing on the rhythm of our steps or the twinkling constellations above, we can attune ourselves to the present moment, silencing the mental chatter and creating space for introspection.

In addition to reconnecting with nature, we must also deliberately cultivate our connection with our inner selves. This process involves actively seeking self-awareness and self-understanding, exploring our values, passions, and dreams. Practices such as journaling can be instrumental in this regard, allowing us to express our thoughts and emotions openly and without judgment.

Mindful meditation is another powerful tool for internal connection. By sitting quietly and focusing on our breath, we can observe our thoughts without becoming entangled in them, fostering a sense of inner peace and clarity. This practice not only helps us connect with our inner world but also teaches us to respond to our thoughts and emotions with compassion and understanding, further strengthening our internal connection.

Furthermore, consciously disconnecting from technology at designated times can help us reclaim our mental space. 'Digital detoxes' or 'tech-free days' can provide much-needed respite from the constant barrage of notifications and updates, allowing us to reconnect with our soul.

Reconnecting with nature and our inner selves isn't a one-time task but a continual journey. It's about finding harmony in our daily lives, aligning our digital existence with our need for internal connection.

In the next section, we are exploring strategies for cultivating a balanced mindset in a digital world, paving the path for a more fulfilled, purpose-driven life.

Section 4: Cultivating a Balanced Mindset in a Digital World

The task of cultivating a balanced mindset in a digital world can seem overwhelming, but it's far from impossible. It's about finding harmony amidst the noise, grounding ourselves in our authentic selves, amidst the flux of digital interactions. Here, we provide a roadmap to help you navigate this journey.

Firstly, it's important to approach technology with intentionality. Be mindful of why you're using a particular app or platform and how it contributes to your life. Limit your use of platforms that don't add value to your life and explore tech tools that aid in personal development, such as meditation apps, digital journals or online learning platforms.

Secondly, establish boundaries around your tech use. Dedicate specific times for checking emails or social media, and avoid screens during certain hours, like before bedtime. These boundaries not only help reduce the constant influx of information, but also provide structured 'quiet periods' for self-reflection and introspection.

Thirdly, engage in regular digital detoxes. These breaks from technology give your mind the space to decompress and reconnect with your inner self. Use this time for activities that foster self-awareness and self-growth, such as journaling, meditation, or mindful walks in nature.

Fourthly, practice mindful technology use. Be fully present during your digital interactions. This not only enhances the quality of these interactions but also reduces the risk of mindless scrolling, helping you redeem your time and mental energy.

Lastly, adopt a gratitude practice. In a world that often focuses on what's missing, gratitude helps us recognize and appreciate what we already have. A daily gratitude journal can be a powerful tool for fostering positivity and internal connection.

Cultivating a balanced mindset in a digital world is an ongoing journey, not a destination. It's about continual growth and adjustment, learning to navigate the ever-evolving digital landscape with mindfulness, intentionality and authenticity.

In the next section, we are gonna wrap up our discussion, summarizing key insights and providing actionable steps to help you embark on this transformative journey.

Conclusion and Action Steps

In this digital age, the challenge of maintaining our internal connection amidst the cacophony of notifications, messages and updates is real. But, as we have explored in this chapter, it's not insurmountable. Through intentionality, mindfulness and a commitment to self-discovery, we can cultivate a balanced mindset and regain our connection with our inner selves.

Remember, the paradox of modern connectedness is a societal challenge, not a personal failing. It's a manifestation of the world we live in, but it doesn't define who we are or who we can become. With deliberate effort and persistence, we can navigate this digital labyrinth, emerging as more grounded, self-aware, and connected individuals.

As we conclude this chapter, here are five actionable steps you can take to start your journey towards internal connection in a digital world:

Intentionality: Evaluate your digital habits. Identify the apps or platforms that add value to your life and those that don't. Consider reducing your use of platforms that don't serve your growth or happiness.

Boundaries: Establish tech-free zones or periods in your day. Use this time for introspection or activities that foster self-growth.

Digital Detox: Dedicate a day or weekend for a digital detox. Disconnect from your devices and reconnect with your inner self and the world around you.

Mindfulness: Practice mindful tech use. Be fully present during your digital interactions and resist the urge to mindlessly scroll. Also, be aware of how your digital interactions may affect others.

Gratitude: Start a daily gratitude journal. Each day, write down three things you're grateful for. This practice helps cultivate a positive mindset and fosters internal connections.

By embracing these practices, you can transform your relationship with technology, fostering a deeper connection with your inner self. Remember, this journey is about progress, not perfection. It's about taking small, consistent steps towards a more balanced, connected and fulfilled life.

You're not alone in this journey. You are seen, you are valued and you have the power to create a life of balance and bliss amidst the digital chaos.

Chapter 4

Cultivating Contemplation: Reclaiming Leisure Time

As we continue our journey, we find ourselves at a critical juncture, where we start acknowledging the need for more profound contemplation in our daily lives.

Remember Walter Mitty from the 2013 movie "The Secret Life of Walter Mitty"? Walter, an employee at Life magazine, finds himself caught in the mundane routines of his day-to-day life. He often escapes into a world of daydreams, embarking on adventures that seem far removed from his reality. However, throughout the movie, Walter discovers that he can cultivate these daydreams into meaningful introspection, helping him break free from his routine and embark on a real-life adventure.

Much like Walter, many of us today are yearning for an adventure, a journey of self-discovery and deeper connection with our inner selves. However, the constant barrage of digital distractions seems to be pulling us away from our true calling. This struggle mirrors a world event that's increasingly gaining momentum - the movement towards digital minimalism. People are starting to realize the need to declutter their digital lives, to make room for introspection and personal growth.

In this chapter, we will explore the dichotomy between doing and contemplation, drawing parallels from Walter's journey and the growing trend of digital minimalism. We are going to delve into the importance of introspection in modern life, finding balance in our leisure activities and strategies to cultivate contemplation in our daily lives.

The promise for you, dear reader, is to equip you with the understanding and tools needed to reclaim your leisure time, foster introspection and create a space for contemplation amidst the hustle of your tech-saturated life.

Section 1 - The Culture of Doing vs Contemplating Creation

In our contemporary society, the culture of doing often takes precedence over the culture of contemplation. We are in a perpetual state of busyness, always striving to accomplish more, to tick off tasks from our never-ending to-do lists. This ceaseless activity is fuelled and further compounded by our digital lives, where instant gratification and the fear of missing out (FOMO) drive us to constantly engage with our devices. The culture of doing is loud, demanding and in your face.

Contrast this with Walter Mitty's daydreams. Each daydream was an island of contemplation in his sea of routine tasks, a space where he could explore his desires, fears and aspirations. His daydreams were not mere flights of fancy; they were a reflection of his inner self, a manifestation of his craving for adventure and fulfillment. This is the power of contemplation - it brings to the surface our deepest desires, enabling us to connect with our true selves.

However, the world we live in doesn't often value contemplation as much as it values action. We're constantly bombarded with messages urging us to do more, be more. This culture of doing has its merits, allowing us to achieve our goals, fulfill our responsibilities and make tangible progress. But in the process, we risk losing touch with our inner selves. We may become like Walter before his adventure - mechanically going through the motions of life without truly living it.

Now, consider the growing movement of digital minimalism. This worldwide trend acknowledges the downside of our hyper-connected digital lives and promotes a more balanced approach. Digital minimalists advocate for intentional use of technology, carving out time for contemplation amidst the culture of doing. It's a call to reconnect with our inner selves, to discover and pursue what truly matters to us.

As we journey through this chapter, we are going to explore how you can cultivate a culture of contemplation in your own life, discuss strategies and exercises that will help you reclaim your time, silence the digital noise and create a space for introspection and personal growth.

Section 2 - The Importance of Introspection in Modern Life

Our modern life can often feel like a whirlwind, where days blend into weeks, weeks into months, and we are left wondering where time has gone. The ever-present digital distractions compound this feeling of being lost in time, making it even more critical for us to cultivate introspection.

Introspection, the act of looking inward, assessing our thoughts, emotions and reactions is a powerful tool for personal growth. Just as Walter Mitty's daydreams allowed him to explore his desires and fears, introspection allows us to delve deeper into our psyche, revealing insights about our habits, behaviors and the things that truly matter to us.

Introspection is an antidote to the mindless scrolling and constant bombardment of information that we experience in the digital world. It allows us to pause, reflect, and make sense of our experiences. It enables us to understand our reactions to different situations, helping us manage our emotions better. Introspection is a pathway to self-awareness, a vital component of emotional intelligence and a key factor in personal and professional success.

Moreover, introspection helps us foster empathy, improving our relationships with others. When we understand ourselves better, we can understand others better too. It creates a foundation for open communication, mutual understanding and stronger connections.

In the context of digital minimalism, introspection plays a crucial role. It involves assessing our digital habits, understanding how they affect our mental and emotional wellbeing and making intentional decisions about our use of technology. It's about choosing to engage with technology in a way that adds value to our lives, rather than depleting it.

As we navigate through this chapter, we are going to explore how you can incorporate introspection into your daily routine, helping you lead a more balanced, fulfilled, and purpose-driven life.

Section 3 - Finding Balance in Leisure Activities

Leisure time is a treasure in our fast-paced, always-on world. It's a chance to unwind, replenish our energy and engage in activities that bring us joy. However, in our digitally dominated lives, leisure time often translates into screen time. We scroll through social media, binge-watch shows or play online games. While these activities can be fun and relaxing, they can also leave us feeling drained and disconnected from our true selves.

Let's revisit Walter Mitty's journey. In the beginning, Walter's leisure time was consumed by his daydreams. However, as he embarked on his real-life adventure, he discovered the joy of engaging in meaningful activities. He found balance by immersing himself in experiences that were in sync with his inner desires and aspirations.

Finding balance in our leisure activities is about creating a blend of digital and non-digital experiences. It's about choosing activities that not only entertain us but also allow us to connect with ourselves and others on a deeper level. This could be reading a book, taking a nature walk, practicing mindfulness or pursuing a hobby.

Balance in leisure activities is a key aspect of digital minimalism. It's about being intentional with our time, choosing to engage in activities that align with our values, and contribute to our personal growth. It's about reclaiming our leisure time from the grip of digital distractions and using it to nurture our mind, body and soul.

In the upcoming section, we'll explore various strategies to help you find balance in your leisure activities, enabling you to create meaningful experiences that enrich your life.

Section 4 - Strategies for Cultivating Contemplation in Daily Life

Navigating through our hyperconnected world might make the idea of cultivating contemplation feel like a challenging endeavor. However, much like our companion in reflection, Walter Mitty, it is possible for us to reclaim our mental space and stimulate deep introspection. Let's delve into how we can weave this into the fabric of our lives.

We begin with a practice that can be seen as the cornerstone of digital minimalism - the digital detox. A detox doesn't need to be an elaborate vacation from technology, it can start as simple and manageable breaks, an hour in the morning, during lunch or before retiring for the night. This time becomes a sanctuary for contemplation and introspection, a brief reprieve from the digital noise that is so often deafening.

However, our goal is not to eliminate technology, but to use it intentionally, which requires mindfulness. Becoming mindful of our relationship with technology involves recognizing our digital habits, including when and why we instinctively reach for our devices. Is it due to boredom, stress, or simply out of habit? Discerning these patterns becomes the first step on the path of transformation.

While we engage in this mindful practice, it becomes beneficial to document our journey, which can be beautifully done through journaling. A journal becomes a mirror reflecting our thoughts, emotions and experiences. It serves as a gateway to our inner world, encouraging introspection and fostering self-awareness. This could take the form of a daily journal or a gratitude journal, where we reflect on the highlights of our day, our feelings or simply things we are grateful for.

Alongside these practices, one must not overlook the power of age-old wisdom in the form of meditation and mindfulness. These practices anchor us in the present moment, enabling us to observe our thoughts without judgment. Even a few minutes of this mindful presence every day can cultivate a deep sense of inner calm and clarity.

Lastly, we must consider the tranquility offered by the natural world. Spending time in nature can be incredibly therapeutic, providing a serene environment to disconnect from the digital world and connect with our inner selves. When taking strolls in nature, we have the opportunity to reflect on our experiences, dreams and aspirations.

The essence of these strategies aligns with the principles of digital minimalism. The idea is not about eradicating technology from our lives, but about using it consciously and intentionally. It's about creating a balance that allows space for contemplation, introspection and personal growth.

Conclusion and Action Steps

As we conclude this chapter, we hope you have a deeper understanding of the importance of introspection and contemplation in our modern, digitally dominated lives. Much like Walter Mitty, each one of us can embark on a personal journey of self-discovery, provided we make time for introspection and foster a culture of contemplation.

In the realm of digital minimalism, the goal is not to completely do away with technology but to use it mindfully and intentionally. It's about making our digital lives serve us, rather than the other way round. This balance enables us to reclaim our leisure time, turning it into a source of joy, personal growth and deeper connections.

Now, let's translate this understanding into action. Here are five steps to get you started on your journey to cultivate contemplation:

Digital Detox: Schedule short technology-free periods in your day. Use this time for contemplation, introspection or engaging in non-digital leisure activities.

Mindful Technology Use: Start noticing your digital habits. When do you reach for your devices? What triggers this behavior? This awareness is the first step towards mindful technology use.

Journaling: Begin a journaling practice. Start by writing about your day, your thoughts, emotions and experiences. Over time, explore themes that emerge in your journal entries.

Meditation and Mindfulness: Begin a daily practice of meditation or mindfulness, even if it's just for a few minutes to start. Use this time to observe your thoughts and emotions without judgment.

Nature Walks: Make time for regular nature walks. Use this time to disconnect from the digital world and connect with your inner self.

Remember, this is a journey, not a destination. Take one step at a time, and don't rush. Progress might be slow, but as long as you're moving forward, you're on the right path.

Chapter 5

Nurturing Relationships in the Digital Era

In the midst of a world constantly pulsating with digital signals, where your next interaction is just a swipe or click away, it becomes imperative to revisit our understanding of relationships. In this chapter, we dive into the unique dynamics of nurturing relationships in the Digital Era.

Consider the film "Her" (2013), a poignant narrative that encapsulates our era's disconcerting realities. The protagonist, Theodore Twombly, navigates a futuristic Los Angeles landscape while grappling with his emotional isolation. His deeply personal, intimate relationship with an artificial intelligence named Samantha portrays the extremes of our tech-oriented lives. It underscores the profound, sometimes unnerving impact of technology on our ability to connect, understand and empathize with one another.

Reflecting on this cinematic allegory allows us to draw parallels with a well-known world event: the rise of social media and digital communication platforms. These technological advancements, akin to the futuristic world of "Her", have significantly transformed the dynamics of human relationships. The advent of social media and dating apps has made it easier for people to connect, but it has also created a space for surface-level interactions, ultimately challenging the depth and authenticity of our connections.

As we venture into this chapter, we promise a journey of discovery and introspection. It's an exploration of the complex intersection between our relationships and the digital platforms that facilitate them. By understanding these dynamics, you can begin to nurture meaningful connections in this digital age, while preserving your own peace and personal growth.

This chapter unfolds in four primary sections:

The broken family and the loss of family values: Here, we are going to delve into how digital distractions have disrupted traditional family structures and values.

The illusion of the complete orange: Empowerment and relationships: This section explores the concept of wholeness within oneself and its impact on forming healthy, fulfilling relationships.

Relationships in the age of social networks and dating apps: We discuss the influence of social media and dating platforms on contemporary relationships, highlighting both the opportunities and challenges they present.

Instant gratification and the erosion of family values: In this section, we are going to analyze the culture of immediacy propagated by the digital era, analyzing its detrimental effects on our relationships and family values.

We are concluding with a summary of the chapter's main points and actionable steps for you to integrate these insights into your daily life. Embrace the opportunity to embark on a journey of self-discovery, as we strive to find balance and build deeper connections amidst the digital cacophony of our lives.

Section 1:The broken family and the loss of family values

Our first section explores the ramifications of our digital age on familial structures and values, a critical facet of human society that's seen unprecedented changes in recent times. These intimate ties, once fostered in the warmth of shared stories and lessons imparted across generations, now compete with the hypnotic lure of screens.

Remember how in "Her," Theodore's interactions with his ex-wife and friends appear diluted in the face of his newfound connection with Samantha, the AI? His emotional reliance on a piece of technology exemplifies the broken families and the loss of family values we witness today. The traditional human bond seems to be dissipating, making way for a new, virtual bond that's more about convenience and less about emotional depth.

Similarly, the increasing prevalence of technology in our real world has led to a profound shift in family dynamics. Dinner tables, once brimming with conversations, laughter and shared experiences, are now often eerily silent, with family members engrossed in their personal digital universes. This shift symbolizes a profound loss of family values, a crucial component of personal development and society's very fiber.

The modern obsession with screens has eroded the time-honored tradition of shared experiences that are key to fostering familial bonds. The loss of such interpersonal connections and shared experiences can stifle our personal growth and limit our emotional repertoire.

As Theodore drifted away from human relationships and deeper into his relationship with Samantha, we saw his emotional world shrink. He alienated those who mattered, trading human connection for a seductive digital illusion. This narrative serves as a mirror to our reality, where technology often disrupts the equilibrium of our family lives.

However, the situation isn't beyond salvage. By consciously acknowledging the influence of technology and fostering healthy boundaries with it, we can begin to mend these fractures. Therein lies our promise to you in this chapter: a pathway to reclaiming the warmth of human connections and grounding our relationships in the shared essence of human experience.

Section 2:The illusion of the complete orange: Empowerment and relationships

As we move forward, let's ponder on the allegory of the 'complete orange'. In our pursuit of relationships, we often carry the misconception that we're incomplete without someone else - that we need someone else to fill in our missing pieces, just like two halves of an orange coming together to form a whole. In "Her," Theodore was drawn to Samantha, believing that her presence would complete his lonely existence.

However, this belief, this illusion of the complete orange, can be disempowering. It perpetuates the idea that we're incomplete on our own, leading us to seek fulfillment and validation from external sources. In the digital age, this misconception is even more dangerous, given the plethora of online platforms that can seemingly offer instant connections and validations.

The reality, though, is that we are complete in ourselves. Each of us is a full orange, not a half. Our sense of fulfillment and purpose should emanate from within us, it shouldn´t be reliant on another person or digital validation. Recognizing this truth is an essential part of personal development for fostering healthier, more fulfilling relationships.

Empowerment in relationships begins with the self. It starts with understanding and accepting our complete selves, our strengths, our flaws, our dreams, and our fears. When we acknowledge and appreciate our inherent completeness, we start forming relationships that complement our lives rather than complete them.

As we navigate the terrain of personal relationships in this digital age, understanding the illusion of the complete orange becomes critical. Just like Theodore, we might find ourselves falling into the trap of seeking completion in external entities, whether it's a person or a digital interface. By acknowledging our inherent completeness, we can form healthier relationships that resonate with our true selves rather than leaning on others for validation or a false sense of wholeness.

However, a critical note of caution as we step onto this path of empowerment: there's a crucial distinction between being a whole orange and falling into the trap of narcissism, led astray by one's ego. Do not misunderstand this call for self-fulfillment and autonomy as an invitation to egotism or self-absorption.

Recognize your inherent completeness. Foster relationships that respect and nurture your individuality rather than consuming it. Be aware of the interfaces that promise quick fixes to your loneliness or insecurity. They are but mirages in the digital desert, unable to quench your thirst for authentic connection and self-discovery.

Section 3: Relationships in the age of social networks and dating apps

In this section, we are delving into the fascinating and somewhat paradoxical world of social networks and dating apps, where relationships often start with a swipe or a click.

The portrayal of relationships in "Her" was startling, yet not entirely alien to us. In many ways, Theodore's romance with Samantha mirrored the manner in which digital relationships are formed today. He did not meet Samantha in a conventional way; their relationship blossomed through constant interactions, much like how relationships develop on social networks and dating apps.

This phenomenon paints a nuanced picture of human connection in our contemporary era. On the one hand, these platforms have democratized social interactions, making it possible for individuals to connect across geographical boundaries, bypassing traditional constraints of time and space. They've made it easier for people to find others with similar interests, ideologies, and life experiences, thereby creating a diverse and global community of digital citizens.

Yet, on the other hand, these platforms also pose unique challenges. While they enable swift connections, they can also develop superficiality. It's easy to cultivate an idealized image online, thus breeding relationships built on carefully curated personas rather than genuine selves. The authenticity and depth that are vital to meaningful relationships may be sacrificed for the sake of digital convenience and appearances.

Additionally, the abundance of choices on these platforms can lead to decision paralysis, a phenomenon where having too many options hampers our ability to make a choice. This can cultivate a sense of dissatisfaction and constant pursuit for 'something better,' thus undermining the stability of relationships.

Indeed, while digital platforms offer convenience and immediate connection, it's crucial to remember that relationships are more than a series of interactions – they are a journey. And just like any journey, they involve ups and downs, twists and turns, conflict and resolution. In fact, relationships often grow and strengthen through conflict. It takes time, effort and patience to develop and find conflict-solving dynamics that work within our relationships.

Consider the virtual relationship between Theodore and Samantha in "Her." Despite being an unconventional relationship, it wasn't devoid of conflict. And yet, these conflicts brought them closer, facilitated deeper understanding, and catalyzed personal growth.

In the digital world of swipes and clicks, the nuances of conflict resolution can easily get lost, thereby leading to superficial relationships. So, it becomes imperative that we intentionally nurture the conflict-solving dynamics in our digital relationships, as much as we do in our real-life relationships.

Section 4: Instant gratification and the erosion of family values

Despite these complexities, it's crucial to remember that these platforms are tools. They hold the potential to both connect and disconnect, to deepen relationships or to create chasms. The key lies in our ability to use these tools consciously, keeping our quest for authentic connection and personal growth at the forefront.

Remember Theodore's journey, where an unconventional relationship illuminated his inner emotional landscape and use that understanding to navigate the complex world of digital relationships. Be mindful of the traps of superficiality and inauthenticity and cherish the connections that resonate with your true self.

Our final exploration takes us into the heart of one of the most challenging aspects of our digital era: the culture of instant gratification and its influence on our relationships and family values.

The fast-paced digital world has set the stage for a culture of immediacy, where everything we desire, whether it's food, entertainment, or even relationships, is available at the click of a button. The subtle narrative of "Her" portrayed how instant gratification, in the form of Samantha's ever-attentive presence, resulted in Theodore neglecting his real-world relationships.

In our contemporary society, instant gratification is often glorified. However, it erodes the virtue of patience and the value in cultivating and nurturing relationships over time. Much like how a gardener tends to a plant, watching it grow from a seedling into a robust tree, relationships also require time, patience and nurturing.

The culture of instant gratification, promoted by the ceaseless stream of notifications and real-time responses, can lead us to take our relationships for granted. In our rush for instantaneous responses, we might overlook the depth of understanding, the shared experiences and the mutual growth that come with time and patience in relationships.

Moreover, the constant demand for immediate responses and interactions can disrupt the harmony of family life, often leading to unnecessary stress and misunderstandings. It erodes the very essence of family values – understanding, patience and mutual respect.

However, remember, we are not powerless. We have the ability to create boundaries, to choose patience over immediacy, depth over surface-level interactions. By consciously choosing to resist the push for instant gratification, we can foster healthier and more meaningful relationships. It's not an easy journey, but it's one that reaps immense rewards.

As we navigate through our digitally dominated lives, it is essential to remember Theodore's journey and the lessons it imparts. We must strive to resist the culture of instant gratification, cultivating the values of patience, understanding and mutual growth in our relationships.

Conclusion and action steps

In conclusion, this chapter delves into the intricate interplay between our personal relationships and the digital age. We've navigated through broken family values, the illusion of completeness in relationships, the complexity of forming connections on social networks and dating apps and the culture of instant gratification.

In the movie "Her," Theodore's life was a microcosm of the relationship dilemmas many of us face today. His journey illuminated the challenges we experience, offering poignant lessons on navigating the tumultuous sea of human connections in the digital era.

Your journey towards authentic connection, however, doesn't end here. These insights and reflections are stepping stones on your path. Let's cement this understanding with five action steps that will guide your way:

Self-reflection: Reflect on your relationship with technology. How does it impact your interactions with your family? How can you balance the digital and physical worlds to foster stronger familial bonds?

Embrace Completeness: Understand and internalize the idea of 'complete orange'. Remember, you are complete in yourself. Embrace your individuality and base your relationships on mutual respect and growth, rather than the need for completion or validation.

Authentic Connection: As you engage with others on digital platforms, strive for authenticity. See beyond curated personas and seek connections that resonate with your genuine self.

Resist Instant Gratification: Cultivate patience and understanding in your relationships. Resist the urge for instant results and cherish the value of nurturing relationships over time.

Set Boundaries: Develop healthy boundaries with technology. Determine dedicated 'no screen' times, especially around family interactions and self-time.

Dare to Grow Through Conflict: Rather than sidestepping conflict or recoiling from it, perceive each dispute as an opportunity for growth. Seek out effective conflict resolution dynamics within each relationship. It's through the crucible of conflict that our relationships gain strength, fostering resilience and deep understanding. It is important to say that we always require ¨Timing¨, respect and empathy to reveal our points of view.

Remember, as we strive for personal growth and purpose, our relationships form a crucial part of our journey. Nurturing these relationships, especially in a digital world, requires conscious effort, patience and understanding.

Your journey is unique, and so are your relationships. Treat them with the care they deserve and watch yourself grow as you tread along this path. As you embark on this exciting voyage of rediscovery, remember: authentic connection begins with you.

Chapter 6

Spirituality and Purpose in a Tech-Dominated World

There is an evocative scene in the 1999 movie "The Matrix", where the protagonist, Neo, is given a choice by the enigmatic Morpheus: take the blue pill and continue living in blissful ignorance, or take the red pill and see reality for what it truly is, a computer simulation designed to keep humanity complacent. It was a definitive moment, a tug-of-war between two worlds, between the comfort of the known and the harrowing truth of the unknown.

This scenario resonates with the modern urbanite's struggle in our tech-dominated society. The rise of digital technology, like the Matrix, has entranced us, drawing us into a realm of endless scrolling, notifications, and superficial interactions. Yet, beneath this digital façade, there lies a deep yearning for meaning, purpose and authentic connection—our red pill moment.

In the same way Neo had to choose between two worlds, you too must make a choice. You can continue existing in a reality dominated by technology, or you can reclaim your autonomy and seek the higher truths within yourself. In this chapter, we are gonna guide you on your journey towards a balanced, purpose-driven life, a journey that harmonizes the technological and the spiritual, the external and the internal.

There are four critical points we will explore in this chapter:

1. The modern man's relationship with spirituality
2. The search for purpose and meaning
3. Finding balance between spirituality and modern life
4. Cultivating a purpose-driven life

Section 1: The Modern Man's Relationship with Spirituality

In the ever-connected, perpetually bustling world of the 21st century, where smartphones act as both compass and timepiece, spirituality often takes a backseat. Amidst the hum of data and the allure of the digital, the modern individuals may feel detached from their spiritual self, viewing it as an abstract concept rather than an essential part of their being.

Yet, beneath this veneer of technological immersion, there exists a latent desire for spiritual fulfillment. It surfaces in quiet moments of reflection, in the hush before dawn, or in the tranquility of a late-night cityscape. Like a river flowing beneath the city streets, it is a persistent reminder of our inherent need for spiritual connection.

Spirituality, at its core, is the relationship we foster with-in ourselves, God, ¨The source¨, the universe, and everything in it. It is a journey of discovery, of introspection, and of understanding. It is our connection to the timeless essence of existence, the realization that we are more than mere flesh and bone, more than just our thoughts, more than the roles we play in the world.

In this digital age, where we're constantly swarmed by an avalanche of information, we often find ourselves lost, disconnected from our spiritual selves. We might perceive spirituality as an extraneous addition to our already packed schedules, or perhaps we may view it as a luxury, reserved only for those with ample time to meditate or go on a soul-searching retreat.

However, spirituality isn't a grandiose concept that requires extensive time or energy. Rather, it is a quiet acknowledgment of our interconnection with the world around us. It is recognizing the symphony in the silence, the wonder in the ordinary, and the sacred in the mundane. Spirituality is the journey towards our authentic selves, a journey that requires us to step beyond the digital veil and embrace our innate human need for purpose, meaning and connection.

Section 2: The Search for Purpose and Meaning

As we step beyond the digital veil and begin our journey of self-discovery, we embark on a path of searching for purpose and meaning. However, amidst the cacophony of societal expectations and self-imposed pressures, finding our purpose can seem like a daunting task.

Purpose isn't merely a career choice or a personal goal—it is the essence of our existence, the driving force behind our actions. It is what makes our hearts beat with passion and our spirits soar with joy. It is, as French philosopher Albert Camus suggests, our rebellion against the absurdity of life, our affirmation of life's intrinsic value.

The tech-dominated world often tempts us to equate success with purpose. We look to external indicators—promotions, likes, followers—for validation and purpose. Yet, such transient rewards can only offer fleeting satisfaction. Our true purpose resides not in the external, but the internal, not in the material, but the spiritual.

Searching for purpose isn't a destination, but a journey, a pilgrimage into the depths of our souls. It isn't a clearly defined path, but an exploration, a series of trials and triumphs that continually shape our understanding of ourselves and the world.

In the words of author and holocaust survivor Viktor Frankl, "One should not search for an abstract meaning of life. Everyone has his own specific vocation or mission in life... Therein he cannot be replaced, nor can his life be repeated." Your purpose, hence, is unique to you. It's a melody only you can sing, a dance only you can perform, a story only you can tell.

Finding purpose in a tech-dominated world may appear counterintuitive. Yet, it is in this very contradiction that we find a paradoxical truth: technology, while often viewed as a distraction, can also be a tool for self-discovery. The same platforms that bombard us with endless notifications can be harnessed to connect with like-minded individuals, to learn new skills, to explore different perspectives and ultimately, to enhance our journey towards self-discovery and purpose. Just as everything in life, the "tool" (technology) is not the problem itself... the problem is the human being dealing with it.

Section 3: Finding Balance between Spirituality and Modern Life

As we journey in search of our purpose, we encounter the essential challenge of modern living: finding balance between our spiritual selves and the demands of the digital world. This balance is not about completely abandoning technology or retreating to the wilderness; instead, it's about harmoniously integrating our spiritual and digital lives.

Just as Neo in "The Matrix" learned to navigate the dualities of his existence, we too must learn to navigate ours. *The key lies not in avoidance, but in awareness.* It's about conscious engagement with technology, using it as a tool rather than letting it use us.

Balance begins with setting boundaries. Our digital devices, while integral to our daily lives, should not dominate our existence. We should control our screen time, not be controlled by it. Consider designating tech-free zones or times in your day. Use these moments for self-reflection, meditation or simply to be present in the world around you.

Remember, *balance is not a static state, but a dynamic process.* It's an ongoing dance between engagement and disengagement, connection and disconnection. It's about aligning our actions with our values and making mindful choices that nourish our souls.

Furthermore, our digital tools can also facilitate our spiritual journey. Apps for meditation or mindfulness, digital journals for self-reflection, online communities for spiritual discourse—all these can enhance our spiritual practice. The key is to *use technology with intention, aligning it with our pursuit of purpose and spiritual growth.*

In the digital age, the line between the physical and the virtual is continually blurring. Yet, amidst this technological evolution, we must hold onto our spiritual core, our inner compass guiding us towards purpose and meaning. Only by striking a balance between our spiritual selves and the digital world can we truly embrace the fullness of our existence.

Section 4: Cultivating a Purpose-Driven Life

Now, having grappled with the dynamics of spirituality, purpose and balance, we turn towards cultivation, towards the active nurturing of a purpose-driven life in this tech-saturated world.

Cultivating a purpose-driven life requires intentionality, the willingness to make conscious decisions aligned with our authentic selves. It's about living proactively rather than reactively, making choices not out of habit, but out of purposeful deliberation.

Start by identifying what truly matters to you. What ignites your passion? What evokes a sense of fulfilment? Your purpose should resonate with your core values, aspirations and passions. It should serve as a guiding star, providing direction amidst the chaos of the digital landscape.

However, living with purpose is more than just acknowledging what we love; it's about integrating this understanding into our daily lives. This is where technology can prove to be an invaluable tool. We can utilize productivity apps to prioritize tasks that align with our purpose, use digital platforms to learn new skills and connect with individuals or communities that share our passions. Yet, a purpose-driven life is not devoid of adversity. There will be moments of doubt, obstacles and setbacks. But it is during these challenging times that our purpose becomes our anchor, providing us with the resilience to weather the storm. Remember, our failures and struggles are not detours from our path but stepping stones along our journey.

In the realm of "The Matrix," Neo discovered his purpose amidst the surreal duality of his existence. He found meaning not in the deceptive comfort of the simulated world, but in the gritty reality of the human struggle. He became the beacon of hope, the embodiment of human resilience and potential.

You too can embody such resilience and purpose. By cultivating a purpose-driven life, you reclaim control from the digital world, navigating it on your own terms. By aligning your actions with your purpose, you experience a deeper sense of fulfilment and connection with your inner self, allowing you to truly thrive in this tech-dominated world.

Conclusion and Action Steps

In this technologically saturated world, finding balance, purpose and cultivating spirituality is a journey, not a destination. It requires conscious engagement, consistent effort and a willingness to explore the depths of your being.

Let's now translate these insights into actionable steps that you can incorporate in your daily life:

Define Your Purpose: Begin by introspecting what truly matters to you. What are your passions, your values, your aspirations? Your purpose is unique to you, so take your time to explore, to question and to understand. A good start is for example to list your values, beliefs, and desires...Now align them into a purpose!

Set Boundaries with Technology: Establish designated tech-free times in your day. Use these periods for self-reflection, meditation, or simply to be present in the world around you. Take time to enjoy the details of life, starting with your morning coffee or beverage. How does it smell? How does it taste?

Utilize Technology with Intention: Harness digital tools to facilitate your spiritual growth and journey towards purpose. Whether it's a meditation app, an online course, or a virtual community, use technology as a tool for self-improvement.

Cultivate Resilience: Recognize that challenges, setbacks and failures are integral parts of your journey. Use them as stepping stones, as lessons that shape your path towards purpose and spiritual growth.

Practice living "Here and Now": Make an effort to be fully present in each moment, to engage with your surroundings consciously and deliberately. Mindfulness serves as a bridge, connecting your spiritual self with the external world.

Like Neo, you have a choice. The blue pill of mindless consumption, digital distractions and superficial engagements or the red pill of purpose, spiritual growth and mindful living. The choice is yours. The path is there, waiting for you to tread, to explore and conquer.

The digital world is not an obstacle to your spiritual journey, but a part of it. It's a labyrinth teeming with challenges, yes, but also with opportunities for growth and self-discovery.

Through this journey, you can transcend the digital chaos, embrace your spiritual self, and cultivate a purpose-driven life. In the marriage of bytes and bliss, of technology and spirituality, you'll find the harmony that lets your soul sing in the symphony of existence.

Chapter 7

Passion and Work in the Digital Age

We live in a world powered by innovation, a world that seems to turn on the axis of technology. This fast-paced digital era, characterized by a flurry of notifications and the constant hum of data transfer, has transformed the fabric of our existence, including our professional lives. In this digital age, our relationship with work has undergone a radical transformation, raising significant questions about passion, purpose and personal development.

Reflecting on the narrative of "Steve Jobs" (2015), directed by Danny Boyle, the nuances of passion and work in the digital age come to life. In the film, Jobs, brilliantly portrayed by Michael Fassbender, is depicted as a man driven by relentless passion, a visionary whose work was not merely a job, but an expression of his very being. This undying passion for innovation, albeit punctuated by significant personal and professional challenges, powered the creation of groundbreaking technology that would revolutionize our world. Similarly, the rise of remote work and digital nomads represents a transformative shift in our understanding of work, prompting us to reassess traditional models and embrace innovative possibilities.

This chapter promises to shed light on the complexities of navigating passion and work in this digital age. The lessons from Jobs' journey and the global transition towards digital workplaces offer rich insights that will guide us in understanding the modern man's relationship with work, exploring the balance between passion and work, identifying challenges and opportunities in the modern workplace, and nurturing passion in a technology-driven career. The balance of Bytes & Bliss hinges upon the successful navigation of these elements.

Are you ready to delve into this intriguing journey of self-discovery, personal development and professional fulfillment? Let's embark together, hand-in-hand, as we navigate the digital labyrinth of the modern workplace.

Section 1: The modern man's relationship with work

As we embark on this journey, let's begin by addressing the cornerstone of our exploration: the modern man's relationship with work. Historically, work has been viewed as a means to an end, a necessary task to put food on the table and a roof overhead. However, with the digital revolution, this perspective has been turned on its head. Today, our work can be more than just a paycheck; it can be an expression of our passions and a pathway to personal growth.

Drawing parallels with Steve Jobs' narrative, the Apple founder didn't merely create technology; he pioneered a revolution. He was known not just for his groundbreaking innovations but also for his unwavering passion for design and functionality. His work with Apple was an extension of himself, his philosophies and visions. Jobs wasn't just creating a product; he was creating an experience, a way of life. He once said, "The only way to do great work is to love what you do." This belief reflects the profound shift in our relationship with work: from a mundane task to a passionate endeavor.

The rise of remote work and the digital nomad lifestyle further reinforces this shift. These work modalities are not just about location independence; they represent a newfound freedom to pursue work that aligns with individual passions, values, and lifestyle preferences. This shift allows the modern worker to seek jobs and projects that resonate with their purpose and provides them with a sense of fulfillment, leading to a more harmonious work-life balance.

However, this new relationship with work is not without its challenges. The blurred boundaries between work and personal life, the constant connectivity and the risk of digital fatigue are all pertinent issues. Yet, they also offer an opportunity to reassess our relationship with work, redefine our priorities, and rekindle our passions.

As we venture deeper into this chapter, we are going to explore these nuances further. We are gonna learn to strike a balance between our passion and work in the digital age, understand the challenges and opportunities that the modern workplace presents and discover ways to nurture our passions in a technology-driven career.

Section 2: Balancing passion and work in a digital world

Balancing passion and work in a digital world is a task that requires introspection, flexibility and a strong sense of self. This balance is a delicate dance, a constant negotiation between the demands of the digital world and the whispers of our soul. It involves leveraging technology as a tool to fuel our passions, rather than allowing it to dictate the course of our professional lives.

Once again, Steve Jobs serves as an inspiring example. Jobs' unparalleled success wasn't a result of blind luck or simple business acumen, but rather his unwavering commitment to his passions. Despite the countless obstacles he faced, Jobs never lost sight of his passion for innovation and design. He leveraged technology not merely as a tool, but as a canvas to bring his visions to life, proving that passion and work can exist in harmony in the digital age.

Jobs' philosophy of following one's passion is reflected in the culture of remote work and digital nomads, which emphasizes the importance of passion-driven work. This work culture encourages individuals to break free from traditional constraints and seek out opportunities that align with their passions and values. The digital world has opened up a universe of possibilities, allowing us to connect with like-minded individuals and organizations that value our unique skills and passions.

Yet, achieving this balance is not always straightforward. In a world where we're constantly bombarded with digital stimuli, it's easy to lose touch with our inner selves and forget what truly ignites our passion. We must be mindful to not let the fast-paced digital world sway us from our true path. It is crucial to take regular digital detoxes, invest time in self-reflection and rekindle our passions, ensuring they remain at the forefront of our professional endeavors.

Section 3: Challenges and opportunities in the modern workplace

As we progress through this chapter, we are going to delve deeper into these challenges and opportunities and discover ways to nourish our passion in a technology-driven career.

The modern workplace is a vibrant tapestry of challenges and opportunities, a constantly evolving landscape that can be both exhilarating and intimidating. In the heart of this paradox, there lies a tremendous potential for growth, both personally and professionally.

Think back to the movie "Steve Jobs". Jobs faced numerous hurdles in his journey, from internal conflicts within Apple to widespread criticism of his leadership style. Yet, he remained steadfast in his vision, turning these challenges into opportunities for innovation and growth. He didn't shy away from difficult decisions or uncomfortable situations, understanding that they were merely stepping stones on the path to greatness. Jobs' tenacity underscores the importance of resilience in the face of adversity and the power of a positive mindset in transforming challenges into opportunities.

The rise of remote work and digital nomads, while liberating and empowering, also presents its own set of challenges. The blurred boundaries between work and personal life, feelings of isolation and the demands of constant connectivity can be daunting. However, these challenges also provide an impetus for us to reassess our work habits, cultivate mindfulness and develop strategies to manage digital fatigue.

In essence, these challenges provide a fertile ground for growth and transformation. They encourage us to explore innovative solutions, build resilience and develop new skills, fostering our personal and professional development. They push us to step outside our comfort zones and learn to navigate the intricacies of the digital world, thereby enabling us to thrive in the modern workplace.

As we venture further into this chapter, we'll explore strategies to nurture our passions in a technology-driven career, thereby empowering us to master the balance of Bytes & Bliss.

Section 4: Nurturing passion in a technology-driven career

Nurturing passion in a technology-driven career can feel like trying to keep a candle lit in a storm. Yet, just as Steve Jobs demonstrated throughout his career, it's not only possible but vital for our personal growth and professional fulfillment.

Jobs, a man who symbolizes technological revolution, never let the dazzling pace of technological advancements overshadow his core passion. From the sleek aesthetics of the Macintosh to the user-friendly interface of the iPhone, his passion for integrating technology and design always shone through. He harnessed the power of technology to manifest his vision, not letting it dictate his path.

A similar philosophy underpins the digital nomad lifestyle. Despite being enmeshed in technology, digital nomads often pursue careers driven by their passions. The digital tools serve as a means to an end, facilitating work but not defining it. Whether it's graphic designing from a beach in Bali or coding from a cafe in Berlin, the essence lies in using technology to enable their passion-driven work, not in letting it consume their passion.

To nurture passion in a technology-driven career, we must adopt a mindful approach to technology usage. Mindfulness allows us to use technology consciously, being aware of its impact on our time, attention, and well-being. We must learn to set clear boundaries, ensuring that our digital lives don't encroach upon our personal space and time. Regular digital detoxes, time for reflection, and staying connected with our inner selves can also go a long way in maintaining our passion.

Moreover, nurturing passion involves continuous learning and growth. Embrace the vast learning opportunities that the digital world offers. From online courses to webinars and podcasts, use these resources to fuel your passion and enhance your skills.

As we conclude this chapter, we'll recapitulate the key insights we've gleaned and propose actionable steps to integrate them into our lives.

Conclusion and action steps

In this digital era, our relationship with work has evolved, offering both challenges and opportunities. Drawing inspiration from Steve Jobs' journey and the rise of remote work and digital nomads, we explored the balance between passion and work, and how to nurture this passion amidst the demands of a technology-driven career.

Finding the sweet spot between Bytes & Bliss is a journey of introspection, resilience and constant learning. It involves understanding our relationship with work, striking a balance between our passion and professional commitments, turning challenges into opportunities and, most importantly, ensuring that our passion isn't overshadowed by the digital world.

Now, to translate these insights into action, here are five steps to guide you on this journey:

1. *Reflect*: Invest time in understanding your relationship with work. What ignites your passion? How can you align your professional life with this passion?
2. *Balance*: Establish clear boundaries between your work and personal life. Remember, technology is a tool to facilitate your work, not to dictate your life.
3. *Embrace Challenges:* When faced with hurdles, remind yourself of Jobs' resilience. Turn these challenges into stepping stones for growth and innovation.
4. *Nurture Passion*: Take regular digital detoxes, stay connected with your inner self and continually fuel your passion.
5. *Learn*: Leverage the digital world for continuous learning. Enhance your skills, stay updated with the latest trends in your field, and keep your passion alive.

As we conclude this chapter, remember that the essence of Bytes & Bliss lies not in shunning the digital world, but in using it mindfully to nurture our passion, fulfill our purpose and enrich our lives.

Chapter 8

Money Matters: Finding Purpose in Prosperity

The twinkling cityscape of New York, the jungle of steel and glass, the beating heart of capitalism - "The Wolf of Wall Street" paints a picture of a modern man's relationship with money that resonates even beyond the boundaries of the silver screen. Jordan Belfort, portrayed masterfully by Leonardo DiCaprio, a man driven by the relentless pursuit of wealth, demonstrates the intoxicating allure and the deep pitfalls of materialism. But, as we dive into the cinematic portrayal, we shall explore how the glittering facade of Wall Street does not provide the deeper sense of fulfillment we all crave.

At the same time, our world, still recovering from the financial crisis of 2008, has started to witness the rise of a phenomenon - conscious consumerism and social entrepreneurship. More and more people are beginning to question the meaning and purpose behind their earnings and expenditures. This shift is a testament to our collective yearning for a purposeful life, one where money serves a greater good, aligning with our personal values and contributing positively to the world.

In this chapter, we shall navigate the choppy waters of our relationship with money, unearthing the often complex dynamics at play. But remember, you are not alone on this journey. As we explore these depths, I am right beside you, sharing the insights and tools you need to reshape your perspective on prosperity. Through the lens of emotional language and motivational encouragement, we shall embark on this transformational journey.

In Section 1, we are going to examine the modern man's relationship with money, diving deep into our collective consciousness and societal conditioning.

In Section 2, we are going to illuminate the pitfalls of materialism, using the metaphorical mirror of Jordan Belfort's life to see the cracks in the facade of wealth without purpose.

Section 3 brings us to the balanced approach of BEING, HAVING, DOING and SAYING. A model that can help us cultivate financial well-being while ensuring that we stay true to ourselves.

Finally, in Section 4, we are going to forge ahead to cultivate a purpose-driven financial mindset, laying the foundation for a healthier, more fulfilling relationship with prosperity.

Section 1: The Modern Man's Relationship with Money

Money, often perceived as the gateway to happiness and security, has etched itself deeply into the psyche of the modern man. From an early age, we're taught that prosperity is synonymous with success, that our worth is intrinsically tied to our bank balance. This belief, perpetuated by societal constructs, has been further fueled by the digital era, where social media channels constantly bombard us with images of opulent lifestyles and the glamour of riches.

While there's nothing inherently wrong with striving for financial success, it's crucial to remember that money is just a tool. It's an instrument that can amplify our experiences, open doors and provide opportunities. But, as we navigate through this complex web of expectations and desires, it's essential to assess how this relationship with money impacts our sense of self and purpose.

Jordan Belfort's journey in "The Wolf of Wall Street" serves as a striking illustration of this dynamic. Caught in the ravenous pursuit of wealth, Belfort becomes disconnected from his inner values, his sense of self swallowed by his insatiable hunger for material gain. As his financial empire expands, his ethical and moral boundaries shrink, a stark reminder that money without a strong moral compass can lead us astray.

Yet, we are not doomed to walk the same path. Just as we've been conditioned to associate money with success, we can also train ourselves to find meaning and purpose beyond our bank statements. This shift doesn't mean disregarding financial prosperity; instead, it encourages a balanced per-spective where financial success becomes a by-product of our true purpose, not the purpose itself.

As we witness the rise of conscious consumerism and social entrepreneurship, we see glimmers of this shift. We see people leveraging their financial power to effect positive change, aligning their spending and investing habits with their beliefs and values. This movement is not about accumu-lating wealth for the sake of it, but about harnessing the power of money to make a tangible difference.

This transformation is not an overnight journey, but a gradual, conscious shift in perspective. It requires introspection, resilience and an unwavering commitment to personal growth. Remember, as you embark on this journey, you're not alone. As you explore, remember the lessons from Jordan Belfort's life - not as a cautionary tale, but as a mirror that reflects your own potential to find a fulfilling and purposeful relationship with money.

Section 2: Money Without Purpose: The Pitfalls of Materialism

If we turn back to the spectacle of "The Wolf of Wall Street," we can see Jordan Belfort, a man who seemingly had it all. Beneath the gilded surface of lavish parties, exotic cars and sprawling mansions, however, lay a hollow emptiness. For all his monetary wealth, Belfort was spiritually bankrupt, his life devoid of genuine fulfillment and purpose. This, dear friend, is the cautionary tale of materialism run amok.

Materialism, the excessive desire for wealth and material possessions, can be a destructive force if left unchecked. It has a tendency to skew our priorities, replacing our deeper desires and values with the shallow pursuit of accumulation. It can lead us to define our self-worth and success by our material possessions rather than our internal values and growth. In essence, we trade our authentic selves for an illusory sense of happiness.

Belfort's story is not an isolated case. Many of us, caught in the whirlwind of our digitally-driven society, find ourselves locked in a similar cycle. We equate having more with being more, unaware that this equation often results in less—less satisfaction, less fulfillment, less peace.

As we step into the world beyond the cinema, we see the ramifications of this mindset. The environmental degradation, economic disparity and rampant consumerism that we witness today are, in part, an outcome of unchecked materialism. Money and possessions, once tools to enhance our lives, have become our masters, steering us away from the path of purpose and fulfillment.

The rise of conscious consumerism and social entrepreneurship offers a beacon of hope in this scenario. It demonstrates a collective awakening, a realization that money can, and should, serve a greater purpose. Consumers are demanding more than just goods and services; they want their purchases to reflect their values, to contribute to the betterment of society and the planet. Entrepreneurs, too, are weaving social and environmental considerations into their business models, indicating a move towards purposeful prosperity.

As we continue our journey towards personal development and purpose, it's crucial to recognize the pitfalls of unchecked materialism. Remember, the true essence of prosperity lies not in what you have, but in who you are and how you contribute to the world.

Section 3: BEING, HAVING, DOING and SAYING: A Balanced Approach to Financial Well-being

BEING, HAVING, DOING and SAYING - these four facets serve as the cornerstones of a balanced approach to financial well-being. They embody the essential elements that, when integrated, foster a healthier, more fulfilling relationship with money.

BEING refers to the cultivation of your authentic self. It's about recognizing and cherishing who you are at your core, independent of your financial status. It encourages you to cultivate self-awareness, nurture your values and foster a strong sense of self-worth that isn't tied to material possessions or monetary wealth.

HAVING, on the other hand, acknowledges the role of money and possessions in our lives. It understands that financial resources can provide comfort, facilitate experiences and serve as a tool to actualize our goals. However, the focus here is on mindful acquisition - owning and using possessions in a manner that aligns with our values and contributes to our well-being.

DOING emphasizes the power of action. It acknowledges that financial prosperity is often the result of our efforts, decisions and actions. By focusing on purposeful actions that align with our personal values and contribute positively to the world, we can cultivate a sense of fulfillment that isn't solely dependent on financial success.

Lastly, SAYING is about expressing your truth and advocating for what you believe in. It's about using your financial resources to support causes you care about and make a difference in the world. It recognizes that money can be a potent force for good when directed by a purpose-driven heart and mind.

If we look back at the rise of conscious consumerism and social entrepreneurship, we see these four facets at play. Consumers and entrepreneurs are BEING true to their values, HAVING possessions and resources mindfully, DOING things that align with their principles and SAYING what they stand for through their financial choices.

The balanced approach of BEING, HAVING, DOING, and SAYING invites you to look beyond the confines of traditional financial success. It encourages you to define prosperity on your own terms, incorporating your authentic self, your values, your actions and your contributions into the equation.

You, dear friend, have been blessed with unique gifts since the moment of your incarnation, gifts that are meant to be unwrapped and shared with the world. Even the smallest of your contributions can ripple outwards, impacting society and humanity in ways beyond your comprehension. So, I urge you, take the steps, however small, to harness your innate gifts. Remember, your smallest action can cast the largest shadow and your smallest kindness can kindle the greatest change.

Section 4: Cultivating a Purpose-Driven Financial Mindset

Having navigated the complexities of our relationship with money, acknowledged the pitfalls of materialism and explored the balanced approach of BEING, HAVING, DOING and SAYING, we now arrive at a crucial juncture in our journey - cultivating a purpose-driven financial mindset.

In the world of "The Wolf of Wall Street," we witnessed Jordan Belfort being devoured by the relentless pursuit of wealth. This was a man who lost sight of his purpose, allowing his financial ambitions to strip away his ethical boundaries and personal values. But again, dear friend, your journey need not follow this path.

A purpose-driven financial mindset is about aligning your financial decisions with your core values and life's purpose. It's about viewing money not as the end goal but as a resource that can help you live a fulfilling life and make a positive impact on the world.

This mindset acknowledges the importance of financial stability and the comfort it brings, but it doesn't stop there. It pushes you to ask deeper questions: How can my financial choices reflect my values? How can my money contribute to my growth and the well-being of others? How can my financial success serve a greater purpose?

These are not easy questions, but they are transformative. They inspire introspection, evoke empathy and provoke a shift in perspective that can fundamentally change your relationship with money.

This mindset echoes the spirit of conscious consumerism and social entrepreneurship, where financial decisions are driven by values and purpose. Whether you're a consumer choosing to buy ethically produced goods, or an entrepreneur integrating social responsibility into your business model, you're embodying a purpose-driven financial mindset.

As you cultivate this mindset, remember that this is a journey of exploration and growth, not perfection. There will be challenges and setbacks, but with every step, every decision, you'll be building a healthier, more fulfilling relationship with money. One that sees financial success not as the destination, but as a vehicle to help you live a purposeful, authentic life.

Conclusion - The Journey Towards Purposeful Prosperity

Our exploration of money, its impact on our lives and our relationship with it, has been a journey full of introspection and insight. We've navigated through the turbulent waters of materialism, drawing lessons from the cinematic spectacle of "The Wolf of Wall Street". We've acknowledged the rise of conscious consumerism and social entrepreneurship, observing the growing shift towards purposeful prosperity. Above all, we've endeavored to redefine our understanding of financial success, moving away from purely materialistic aspirations towards a purpose-driven financial mindset.

This journey is about recognizing the transformative power of purpose in our financial decisions. It's about integrating the facets of BEING, HAVING, DOING and SAYING into our monetary pursuits, thereby fostering a balanced and fulfilling relationship with money. It's about using financial resources not just for self-satisfaction, but for contributing to the greater good, aligning our financial actions with our core values and principles.

As we conclude this chapter, it's essential to remember that the journey towards purposeful prosperity is a continuous process of learning, growth and evolution. It's about staying true to your authentic self, even in the face of societal pressure and digital distractions. It's about exercising the courage to choose the less trodden path, to redefine success on your own terms.

In your journey towards purposeful prosperity, here are five action steps to guide you:

Cultivate Self-awareness: Understand your values, beliefs and desires. Recognize how these influence your financial decisions.

Mindful Acquisition: Assess your consumption habits. Aim to own and use possessions in a manner that aligns with your values and contributes to your well-being.

Purposeful Actions: Align your financial actions with your core values. Let your monetary decisions reflect who you are and what you stand for.

Advocate for Your Beliefs: Use your financial resources to support causes you care about. Leverage your monetary power to effect positive change.

Embrace the Journey: Acknowledge that this is a journey, not a destination. Celebrate your progress and learn from your setbacks. Win or Learn!

With these steps in mind, you're now equipped to embark on the transformative journey towards purposeful prosperity.

Chapter 9

Feeding Mind and Body: The Conscious Man's Guide

In the age of connectivity, we often forget that the most important connection is the one we have with ourselves. We live in a time when the pursuit of material gain often overshadows the nourishment of the mind and body. Today, we step off the relentless treadmill of external achievements to delve into the profound territory of self-care. We venture into the realm of our consciousness and physicality, a journey that shall lead us to better understand the importance of feeding both mind and body in this chaotic digital world.

Take a moment to consider the 2011 film "Limitless". In this tale, Eddie Morra, a struggling writer, stumbles upon a mysterious pill called NZT-48. This "smart drug" not only enhances his intellectual abilities, but also improves his physical health and appearance, leading to unprecedented success. But as the story unfolds, we witness the repercussions of this artificial, unsustainable method of self-improvement. The film subtly reveals an undeniable truth:

there are no shortcuts to true growth and well-being. This is a powerful reminder that what we consume, both mentally and physically, profoundly impacts our well-being.

In parallel, consider the global wellness movement that has transformed the way we perceive health and wellness. It emphasizes a holistic approach, urging us to balance our physical health with our mental and emotional well-being. The rise of practices such as yoga, meditation, and conscious eating mirrors the principles highlighted in this chapter. We are being invited to understand that true health extends beyond the physical and that our thoughts and feelings play a pivotal role in shaping our reality.

We are invited to understand that true health extends beyond the physical body and that our thoughts and feelings play a fundamental role in shaping our reality. This is where quantum medicine opens up a universe of possibilities. This contemporary science maintains that at the cellular level we are 90% empty space, ready to be completed and transformed by our consciousness. This notion revolutionizes our perceptions, showing us that we are not mere physical beings, but conscious beings with the power to influence our own existence at the cellular level. This perspective elevates our understanding of health and wellbeing to a profound and intrinsic level, where our mind and consciousness are active protagonists.

In this chapter, "Feeding Mind and Body: The Conscious Man's Guide to Nourishment", we are going to explore the integral role of conscious nourishment in personal growth and wellbeing. We are going to discover how food is more than mere sustenance; it's a form of medicine that, when chosen consciously, can lead to enhanced health and vitality. We are going to delve into the mind-body connection, exploring how our thoughts can create or distort our reality. Finally, we are going to consider how we can protect ourselves against polar-

ization and close-mindedness by embracing a more thoughtful and conscious approach to life.

By the end of this journey, we will have unpacked four key
themes. These insights shall serve as a compass, guiding you
towards a more mindful, balanced, and purposeful existence.
The road to self-discovery and growth is not free from challenges, but remember: every step you take on this journey
brings you closer to becoming the best version of yourself.

*Section 1:Intellectual and physical nutrition of the
modern man*

We begin our journey by exploring the physical and intellectual nourishment of the modern man. In the heart of
bustling cities, where the symphony of car horns and the
flickering neon lights of billboards hold a relentless concert,
our connection with our bodies and minds can often fade into
the background. The urgency of our daily routines can overshadow the essential act of consciously nourishing our bodies
and minds.

Eddie Morra, in "Limitless", began his journey as an individual grappling with a lack of motivation, sluggish mental
agility and a faltering physical presence. His initial state is
reminiscent of many urban dwellers, lost in the hustle and
consumed by pressures. Like Eddie, many of us might wish for
a magical pill to boost our physical and mental energy. However, the story serves as a stark reminder that shortcuts
seldom lead to long-term success or well-being.

In contrast to this cinematic illustration, real-life success
and wellness are a result of consistent, mindful actions. The
consumption of nutrient-rich food, coupled with intellectual
stimuli that challenge and expand our mental capacity, forms
the cornerstone of this philosophy. As an integral part of the

global wellness movement, nourishing the body and mind is about being mindful of what we consume in our day-to-day lives.

We often underestimate the impact of consciously choosing food (not a fan of calling it "Diet") on our physical health and mental performance. Our bodies, like complex machines, require high-quality fuel to function optimally. Each morsel we ingest impacts our energy levels, our mood, our cognition and overall health. However, physical nourishment extends beyond food; it also includes physical activity, adequate rest and a balance between exertion and relaxation.

Furthermore, physical nourishment implies as well something deeply powerful and often underestimated: conscious attention to the state of our body and the use of that awareness to instruct our body to accompany us all along the way.

Just as quantum medicine teaches us that we are 90% empty space at the cellular level, we must also fill that void with our consciousness, anchored in the present moment. It is not just about nourishing our bodies with the right nutrients, but also infusing every cell of our body with a full awareness of its state, nourishing it with food and our conscious attention and intention. This act of filling the void in our cells with our consciousness is a powerful mindfulness exercise. It is a way to honor our body and ourselves, it is a way to reclaim our personal power and health, and it is a way to affirm our intention to live a full, energetic and healthy life. Above all, it is a constant reminder that we have the capacity and the responsibility to shape our reality, starting from within, at the cellular level.

Intellectual nourishment, on the other hand, goes beyond the academic learning we've been conditioned to value. It is about broadening our horizons, nurturing our curiosity, and stimulating our minds with diverse ideas and experiences. It involves reading widely, engaging in thoughtful conversations

Therefore, it is essential that we choose foods as close as possible to their natural state, minimizing ultra-processed products. When we eat mindfully, we are not only choosing what we eat, but also where it comes from.

Embrace the power of ancient feeding wisdom. Understand that food is more than mere sustenance. It's a form of medicine, a tool for health, vitality and longevity. When we eat mindfully and healthfully, we are not just feeding our bodies; we are nurturing our minds, our spirits and our overall well-being.

Section 3: The mind-body connection: thoughts are energy

As we continue to journey through the realms of conscious nourishment, let's delve into the realm of the mind-body connection. The axiom "mind over matter" takes on a profound significance as we explore how thoughts are energy that creates our reality.

Throughout "Limitless," we see Eddie Morra's mental state drastically alter his physical reality. The NZT-48 pill does not change the world around him but rather alters his perception of it. The fascinating thread in this narrative lies in the fact that the transformation is not solely physical but profoundly mental. When Eddie changes his thoughts and perceptions, he influences his reality.

However, in our lives, the transformative power of thought doesn't require a magical pill. The global wellness movement has increasingly recognized the importance of the mind-body connection in shaping our health and well-being. Modern research supports ancient wisdom, revealing the intricate ways our thoughts and emotions can impact our physical health.

Consider the placebo effect, a phenomenon where a patient's symptoms can be alleviated by an otherwise ineffective treatment, simply because they believe it will work. This demonstrates the potent power our minds wield over our bodies. Similarly, chronic stress, a predominantly psychological issue, can lead to physical problems like hypertension and heart disease. On a positive note, practices such as mindfulness and meditation can have beneficial effects on both mental and physical health, further highlighting the mind-body connection.

Here comes the magic: quantum medicine teaches us that we are 90% empty space at the cellular level, space that can be completed and transformed by our consciousness. Therefore, I invite you to remember this: Consciously fill that 90% of empty space in your cells with gratitude or another positive feelings to keep your body healthy. Feed that void with light, love, well-being. I guarantee your body and mind will thank you.

Embracing the mind-body connection involves acknowledging that our thoughts are not merely abstract phenomena. They are energetic entities that interact with our physical bodies and our world. When we nurture positive thoughts, we create a positive reality for ourselves. When we harbor negative thoughts, we risk manifesting negative outcomes.

The key is awareness. By becoming mindful of our thought patterns, we can actively choose thoughts that align with our aspirations and our desire for good health and happiness. We can shape our reality through conscious thought.

Section 4: Construction of reality through thought and protecting against polarization of ideas

As we navigate our exploration of nourishment, let's address a crucial aspect of our intellectual well-being: our perception of reality. This ties into our exploration of the mind-body connection, but here we are concerned with how we protect ourselves from polarization of ideas, or what we can term as the 'anti-thinking' way.

Throughout "Limitless", Eddie Morra's perception of reality dramatically shifts with the use of the NZT-48 pill. Initially, the altered reality seems thrilling, offering him an unparalleled sense of power and control. However, as the story unfolds, the illusion crumbles, revealing the grave pitfalls of an unbalanced perspective. Eddie's experience stands as a potent reminder of the danger of falling into extreme ways of thinking, be it limitless possibilities or hopeless despair.

In the context of the global wellness movement, polarization of ideas often manifests as rigid beliefs and practices. For instance, certain dietary trends are hailed as the 'ultimate' path to health, ignoring the complexities of individual differences and holistic wellbeing. Alternatively, an over-emphasis on mindfulness can lead to the neglect of physical wellness.

Being conscious of this tendency towards polarization is the first step towards maintaining a balanced perspective. The 'anti-thinking' way is not about shutting down our thinking process, but rather about avoiding extreme or binary ways of thinking. It's about embracing a more nuanced, open and empathetic approach to ideas and experiences.

Developing this mindset involves cultivating curiosity and practicing active open-mindedness. Instead of clinging to specific beliefs or ideas, be open to exploring different perspectives and integrating them in a way that aligns with your personal truth. Engage in dialogues and debates to broaden your understanding and challenge your preconceived notions.

In essence, protecting against polarization involves building intellectual flexibility. Like a tree that bends with the wind, the ability to adapt our thinking to changing circumstances and new information leads to resilience and growth. This approach aligns with the principles of the global wellness movement and supports the idea of food as medicine, encouraging us to remain flexible and open in our pursuit of health and wellbeing.

This section closes our exploration of the conscious man's guide to nourishment. With this foundation, we can move towards living more mindfully and healthfully in our digital world.

Conclusion and action steps

As we draw this chapter to a close, it's essential to distill what we've discussed and how it relates to our journey towards mindful nourishment in the digital world. Much like Eddie Morra's journey in "Limitless," we are constantly presented with opportunities to expand our potential and live more meaningful, enriched lives. The journey, however, is not about finding a magical pill, but about making mindful choices in our nourishment, embracing the interconnectedness of our minds and bodies, and fostering intellectual flexibility to avoid polarization.

We started our exploration with the physical and intellectual nourishment of the modern man, underscoring the importance of balanced, healthful eating and broad intellectual stimulation. We moved on to ancient wisdom about food as medicine, reinforcing the notion that our daily food choices play a pivotal role in our health and well-being.

We then delved into the mind-body connection and the powerful influence of our thoughts on our reality. Lastly, we explored the concept of avoiding polarization of ideas, embracing a balanced and open-minded perspective in our journey towards wellness.

As we look to the future, there are five action steps to integrate these principles into your life:

Conscious Eating: Practice mindful eating. Pay attention to what you eat, how much you eat, when you eat and why you eat. Choose nutrient-dense foods that support your physical well-being. You must pay attention to what your body asks for each time of the day, that it's body awareness my dear friend, that's knowing what your body needs and how it reacts to certain food at certain times.

Intellectual Stimulation: Dedicate time to broaden your horizons. Read widely, engage in meaningful conversations and challenge your own beliefs and assumptions. Understand the viewpoint that is diametrically opposed to your current thinking, even if you do not share it; this will test your truth and give you confidence in your final choice.

Embrace the Mind-Body Connection: Foster positive thinking and manage stress through practices such as meditation, biodanza, and streaching. Recognize the influence of your mental state on your physical health. Remember it is your responsibility to fill with emotional health the 90% of the void within your cells.

Avoid Polarization: Maintain an open mind and demonstrate intellectual flexibility. Be open to differing perspectives and avoid rigid thinking. Practice empathetic understanding and always ground your beliefs in your personal values. Remember, it's through this balance that we cultivate a richer understanding of ourselves and the world around us.

Integrate Holistic Practices: Align with the principles of the global wellness movement. Consider integrating holistic health practices into your lifestyle, such as regular physical activity, sufficient sleep and mindfulness practices.

By integrating these steps into your life, you'll be well on your way to mastering the art of mindful nourishment in the digital world, fostering a deeper connection with your inner self, and living a more balanced, fulfilling life. The journey to Bytes & Bliss starts here.

Chapter 10

Practical Guide to Thriving in Modernity

In the acclaimed anthropological work, "The Teachings of Don Juan," author Carlos Castaneda shares a series of conversations with the Yaqui Shaman Don Juan. Through his journeys with Don Juan, Castaneda finds profound wisdom, techniques to perceive the world differently, and strategies to navigate the complexity of life. This spiritual journey mirrors our own in the digital age, although we're not grappling with mystical realms, but a reality saturated with technology.

Our lives, much like Castaneda's, require us to navigate complex environments, which, in our case, are replete with digital distractions. This ever-increasing digitization of life creates a unique and urgent need for personal development and inner growth, just as Don Juan guided Castaneda to unravel his inner self amidst a different kind of complexity.

The recent rise of self-help and personal development resources reflects this collective yearning for purpose and meaning amidst the digital chaos. We're all seekers on our paths, negotiating the labyrinth of technology, while longing for connecting with our authentic selves, much like Castaneda navigating the spiritual realms guided by Don Juan. This chapter promises to be your Don Juan in the context of digital distractions, guiding you to strategies that will empower you to regain control of your life, reconnect with your inner self and foster your personal growth.

In this chapter, we´re going to explore four transformative areas. Firstly, we´re gonna dive into techniques for staying grounded amidst digital distractions. Next, we're gonna delve into nurturing self-awareness and personal growth in a technology-dominated world. Our third aim is to build strong relationships despite the depersonalizing effects of technology. Finally, we're going to embrace purpose, passion and spirituality in this modern era.

This journey is about finding your peace and path amidst the digital noise. It's about nurturing your inner self while navigating the challenges of modernity. Let's begin this journey towards personal mastery in the digital age together.

Section 1: Techniques for staying grounded in a digital world

In a world where screens flash, notifications ping and artificial intelligence surrounds us, the quest to stay grounded can seem like an insurmountable task. Much like Carlos Castaneda in the realms of Don Juan, we must develop strategies and techniques to remain centered amidst the digital chaos.

Firstly, consider the practice of digital detoxification. Like cleansing your body of toxins, a digital detox involves intentionally distancing oneself from digital devices for a set period. This could range from a few hours each day, weekends, or even a full week or more, depending on your comfort level. The purpose is to create a space free from the constant bombardment of digital stimuli, allowing your mind to rest and refocus on the physical world around you.

The second technique involves creating digital boundaries. Establish set times for checking emails, social media and other digital platforms. Resist the urge to respond immediately to every beep, buzz, or flash. These boundaries can help reclaim your time, allowing for moments of reflection and introspection.

Thirdly, engage in mindfulness exercises. These can help you stay present and centered in the midst of digital distractions. Mindfulness practices such as meditation, yoga, or even simply deep, intentional breathing can provide a much-needed grounding influence. You may also use apps designed to aid mindfulness, turning the tide on technology, using them as tools for staying grounded.

Finally, nurture your relationship with nature. Nature provides a calming, grounding influence, a contrast to the artificial, fast-paced digital world. Regular walks in the park, hiking, or simply sitting under a tree can have immense grounding effects.

These strategies are but a beginning, a foundational shift from being subsumed by digital noise to starting to control it. Just like Castaneda had to acclimatize to the realm of Don Juan, this is a process that requires practice and patience. Remember, little changes in our habits make a huge difference in time.

Section 2: Nurturing self-awareness and personal growth

As you begin to establish your digital boundaries, the next crucial step on your journey is fostering self-awareness and personal growth. In Don Juan's teachings, he constantly emphasized the importance of self-awareness, explaining that it was a key step to unlocking one's personal power. Our digital realm, although seemingly different, isn't that different in this context.

Start by acknowledging your relationship with technology. How often are you reaching for your phone? How does it make you feel? Is it a source of stress or does it offer a comfortingly predictable distraction? These questions may seem simple, but they are profound in developing a deeper understanding of your relationship with the digital world.

Next, cultivate mindfulness. By regularly practicing mindfulness, whether through meditation, journaling, or simple mindfulness exercises, you encourage a more profound awareness of your thoughts and emotions. This heightened sense of awareness can help you identify areas in your digital behavior that need addressing, facilitating the transition to healthier digital habits.

Consider also, the practice of intentional digital consumption. Just as you might consider the nutrition of the food you eat, you should consider the digital 'nutrition' of your online activities. Be selective about what you consume. Prioritize content that fosters growth, curiosity, and positivity over mindless scrolling or negative content. When you interact online, do so consciously! Consider how your post or comment will impact others - is it in alignment with your personal values? Acknowledge that your digital interactions will be consumed by others and carry a certain degree of influence. It's not just about what you take from the digital world, but also what you contribute to it. Always remember to engage responsibly, adding to the positivity and growth of the online community.

Lastly, allow yourself to embrace silence and solitude. These are precious commodities in our modern, fast-paced world, yet they provide fertile ground for self-discovery and personal growth. Use your time away from digital devices to introspect, reflect and connect with your inner self.

As Don Juan guided Castaneda to discover his inner power and wisdom, let these practices guide you towards a better understanding of yourself in the digital world.

Section 3: Building strong relationships in a technology-driven society

In a world where connections can be created with a single click, it's crucial to remember that relationships, the meaningful ones, require more than just digital interaction. Don Juan emphasized the importance of interpersonal connections in Castaneda's journeys, a lesson equally applicable in our technology-driven world.

Begin by distinguishing between online connections and real relationships. While social media can provide a sense of connectedness, it is essential to recognize the value of in-person interactions and deep, meaningful conversations. These cannot be replaced by likes, shares or emoji-filled comments.

Actively invest time in cultivating your relationships outside the digital world. Make an effort to meet friends and family members in person, engage in activities together, and have real conversations. This not only strengthens your relationships but also helps to maintain a healthy balance between your digital and physical world.

Prioritize quality over quantity in your connections. A hundred online acquaintances do not equate to one close friend who understands and supports you. Foster deeper connections with a select few, rather than spreading your attention thinly across numerous superficial relationships.

Lastly, be present. It's easy to be physically present yet mentally lost in the digital world. When you're with someone, be with them fully, without the interruptions of digital devices. Consider the importance of eye contact. This present awareness enriches your relationships and helps you connect more deeply with others.

Don Juan taught Castaneda that personal power was intertwined with one's ability to forge strong connections with others and the world around them. In our context, it's about building authentic, meaningful relationships in a society often more focused on digital connections.

Section 4: Embracing purpose, passion and spirituality in the modern era

In navigating modernity, it's vital not to lose sight of the elements that add depth and purpose to our lives. As Don Juan led Castaneda on spiritual quests, we too can embark on our quests for purpose, passion and spirituality amidst the digital hustle.

To begin with, always remember your 'why.' Identify what truly motivates and drives you. What is your purpose? What are your passions? These are the anchors that will keep you grounded amidst the digital noise. Write them down, remind yourself of them daily and use them as a compass to guide your actions and choices. Also, remember we are defined by our "Noes", it's easy to say "Yes" to everything in life, it takes character and awareness of ourselves to know what are our "Noes" in life.

Secondly, seek out digital spaces that align with your purpose and passions. The digital world, though often overwhelming, can also provide opportunities for growth and connection. Follow digital platforms and communities that align with your interests, passions and goals. Use technology to your advantage, not detriment.

Thirdly, incorporate spirituality into your daily routine. Spirituality doesn't necessarily mean religion; it can be anything that helps you connect with your inner self and the world around you on a deeper level. It could be meditation, nature walks, practicing gratitude or engaging in acts of kindness.

Lastly, always stay open to learning and evolving. Don Juan stressed to Castaneda that the path to personal power involved continual learning and adaptation. In our digital age, this translates to keeping an open mind, embracing change and continually seeking ways to grow and evolve.

By doing so, we don't merely survive in the digital world; we learn to thrive, finding our purpose and passion and cultivating a deeper spiritual connection amidst the digital chaos.

Conclusion and action steps

Navigating the modern, technology-driven world, much like Carlos Castaneda's journey with Don Juan, is about finding balance amidst chaos, fostering self-awareness, building strong relationships and nurturing a deep sense of purpose. By implementing the strategies discussed in this chapter, you can begin to regain control of your digital life, foster inner growth and thrive in modernity.

This journey is not about eliminating technology from your life, but learning to coexist with it without losing touch with your inner self. Just as Castaneda learned to find his path amidst the mystical realms, you too can discover your path in our digital world.

Let's recap the steps we covered in this chapter:

Grounding techniques: Adopt practices like digital detoxification, setting digital boundaries, mindfulness and reconnecting with nature.

Nurturing self-awareness: Acknowledge your relationship with technology, practice mindfulness, consume digital content intentionally and embrace silence.

Building strong relationships: Distinguish between online connections and real relationships, invest in cultivating relationships outside the digital world, prioritize quality over quantity and be fully present.

Embracing purpose and spirituality: Remember your 'why,' align your digital spaces with your passions, incorporate spirituality into your daily routine, and stay open to learning and evolving.

The journey ahead shall not be easy, but remember, you have the power to navigate the digital labyrinth, choose personal growth over distractions, and rediscover your true purpose. You are not alone on this journey. With every step you take, you join a collective movement of individuals seeking to reclaim their lives from digital distractions, find their purpose and live authentically now.

Action Steps:

Schedule a digital detox, whether for a few hours, a day, or a week. Schedule it!

Implement a *daily mindfulness* practice. Identify which practice resonates with you.

Plan an *in-person meet-up* with a friend or family member.

Write down *your passions and purpose* and review them daily.

Join an online community that aligns with your passions or interests. You can join our Bytes and Bliss community!

It's time to step into your personal power, finding balance, purpose, and bliss amidst the bytes. This is the first day of a better YOU!

Chapter 11

Rediscovering Balance: Creating a Personal Blueprint for Mindful Living

As the soft hues of the sun dissolve into the dusky twilight, you may often find yourself lost in the sea of bytes. Your heart's yearning for the rhythm of your own existence is drowned by the digital clamor of constant notifications, emails, and superficial interactions. But what if there existed a path, much like the one tread by Elizabeth Gilbert in the heart-touching narrative of "Eat Pray Love," that could lead you to find yourself amidst the digital whirlwind?

In "Eat Pray Love", Gilbert embarks on a journey of self-discovery, as she explores diverse cultures and spiritual practices. Leaving behind her modern life's expectations and distractions, she delves deep into her inner self. Amidst the meditative calm of an Ashram in India, she discovers the art of mindfulness, of living in the present and the joy of genuine human connections.

In this chapter, we aim to help you embark on a similar journey of self-discovery and personal growth. But unlike Gilbert, you need not traverse continents. Your journey will be within the confines of your existing, technology-driven life. You are going to be introduced to the delicate art of balancing bytes and bliss, technology and tranquility, connectivity and consciousness. Just like the increasing global interest in mindfulness and meditation practices, you too will delve into the soothing realm of mindful living, right here, right now.

The digital world, with its overwhelming ocean of information and incessant demands on our attention, can often steer us away from our path to personal growth. But, by developing a mindful relationship with technology, we can reclaim our time, focus, and emotional energy.

We promise to guide you step by step as you explore:

Section 1: Assessing your current relationship with technology. We shall walk with you through the labyrinth of your digital interactions, helping you see the impact of your current usage patterns on your mental and emotional well-being.

Section 2: Identifying areas for improvement and growth. Together, we shall discover the areas in your digital life that can be fine-tuned to serve your personal development goals better.

Section 3: Designing your personal blueprint for mindful living. As an architect of your life, you will learn how to design a life that incorporates technology without being dominated by it.

Section 4: Implementing and refining your plan for balance. You shall learn how to sustain and refine this plan as you evolve, ensuring your digital life remains in service to your personal growth.

Let's embark on this journey together, one that's punctuated with self-reflection, mindfulness and immense personal growth. Remember, just like Gilbert, who found love, happiness and spiritual enlightenment in her quest, your journey, too, holds the promise of incredible transformation.

Section 1: Assessing your current relationship with technology

Imagine you're standing before a giant mirror, not to assess your physical appearance but to take a good, long, hard look at your digital self. This is the first step in our journey together—assessing your current relationship with technology. We start here, to change our relationship with technology, we first need to understand it, acknowledge its presence and comprehend its impact on our lives.

Much like Elizabeth Gilbert, who in "Eat Pray Love," had to face her discontent and restlessness before she could seek the solace of peace and mindfulness. Similarly, you need to confront the digital 'noise' in your life to silence it, to replace it with the 'melody' of mindfulness.

Begin by cataloguing a typical day in your life. How much time do you spend on social media? How often do you check your emails or instant messaging apps? How many hours are you devoting to mindless scrolling or binge-watching? Be brutally honest. Only by embracing the reality of our present can we shape the promise of our future.

Next, introspect on how your digital habits are impacting your emotions. Do you feel an incessant urge to check your phone? Does the thought of missing out on the latest update or news make you anxious? If a significant part of your happiness is tied to your virtual interactions, then you, my friend, are caught in the byte web.

Evaluate how technology is affecting your real-world relationships. Are you truly present when spending time with loved ones, or are you mentally elsewhere, scrolling through your phone? Remember, every byte that disconnects you from the present moment is a byte stealing away your bliss.

Like the global community that has shown a growing interest in mindfulness practices, you too need to reflect upon your digital practices. Is your use of technology serving your personal growth, or is it detracting from it? Consider if the time spent online is aiding you in your journey towards self-fulfillment, or is it merely creating a mirage of connection and accomplishment.

Lastly, let's delve deeper into how your online life aligns with your personal values and aspirations. Is your digital persona a reflection of your authentic self, or have you, like many others, been swept away by the currents of digital conformity and pretense? The goal here is to align your virtual presence with your true essence.

This journey, like Gilbert's, requires courage. It requires the courage to confront the truth, to confront the discomfort of realizing that we might be losing ourselves in the maze of digital distractions. But remember, every moment of honest reflection is a step towards discovering your authentic self amidst the virtual chaos.

Section 2: Identifying areas for improvement and growth

Now that we've held a mirror to your current relationship with technology, let's move on to identifying areas for improvement and growth. Remember, this is not about pointing out flaws or criticizing our digital habits; it's about understanding where we stand and where we can possibly move towards betterment, towards the bliss we so earnestly desire.

Just as Elizabeth Gilbert in "Eat Pray Love" sought growth in Italy's delectable cuisine, India's spiritual retreats and Bali's human connections, we too must seek growth, within our daily digital interactions. Each platform, each app, each technological tool can become an opportunity for growth if we approach it mindfully.

Start by identifying the digital activities that contribute the most to your distractions or disconnections. Is it a social media platform that keeps you hooked with endless scrolling? Or a gaming app that makes hours fly like minutes? High-lighting these 'problem areas' will provide you with a clear idea of where to direct your efforts for change.

Then, consider the moments when technology tends to disrupt your peace or intrudes on your 'me' time. Is it the work emails pinging after office hours? Or the late-night notifications that disrupt your sleep? Recognizing these instances of digital intrusion shall help you create a healthier and more balanced tech-life boundary.

In this global age of mindfulness, people worldwide are taking strides to reduce their digital distractions. The next step for you is to ponder upon how your digital habits align with your personal development goals. Are these habits empowering you to be the person you aspire to be, or are they holding you back?

Next, observe how often your online engagements are intentional versus impulsive. Are you spending time online out of habit or boredom, or are you mindfully choosing to engage with purposeful content that enhances your growth?

Lastly, think about the opportunities for real-world experiences and personal growth that you might be missing out on due to excessive screen time. Are there hobbies, relationships or experiences that you've been neglecting? Realizing what you might be sacrificing at the altar of technology can be an eye-opening experience.

By introspecting on these aspects, we have identified areas in your digital life that need fine-tuning to serve your personal development goals better. Just as Gilbert found opportunities for growth in the most unexpected corners of the world, we too can find opportunities for growth within our byte-driven lives.

Section 3: Designing your personal blueprint for mindful living

Now that we've assessed our current relationship with technology and identified areas for improvement, it's time for you to design your personal blueprint for mindful living. Just like Elizabeth Gilbert created her own unique path to mindfulness in "Eat Pray Love," you, too, will carve out a personalized journey to balance and bliss in the digital world.

The first step to designing your blueprint is to outline your vision for a balanced digital life. What does mindful tech usage look like to you? Is it having specific times to disconnect every day? Or setting aside screen-free weekends? Maybe it's being fully present in your real-world interactions or simply not feeling compelled to capture every moment for social media. Visualize this ideal state of digital equilibrium and make it the cornerstone of your blueprint.

Next, set tangible and achievable goals that align with this vision. These goals could be reducing your screen time by an hour each day, dedicating specific periods for uninterrupted focus, or designating tech-free zones in your home. Remember, the intention is not to completely eliminate technology, but to create a more mindful and purpose-driven relationship with it.

Following the trend of the growing global interest in mindfulness practices, you might want to include meditation or digital detox practices in your blueprint. Such practices can help cultivate mental clarity and focus, empowering you to use technology in a more controlled and conscious manner.

Furthermore, consider how you can use technology to aid your personal growth. Are there apps or platforms that can contribute to your knowledge, skills or wellbeing? Just like Gilbert used language learning resources in Italy or yoga practices in India, find digital tools that can enhance your journey towards self-fulfillment.

Lastly, integrate strategies for sustaining your blueprint over time. Life is ever-changing and so is the realm of technology. Your blueprint should be flexible, evolving as you grow and as new technologies emerge. Regularly assess your tech habits, tweak your goals and, most importantly, celebrate your progress—no matter how small.

Remember, this blueprint is not a rigid roadmap but a guiding compass. It's meant to navigate you through the digital world without losing sight of your inner world. As you pen down this blueprint, you are scripting a new narrative for yourself, one where bytes and bliss coexist harmoniously.

Section 4: Implementing and refining your plan for balance

With your personal blueprint in hand, you're ready to implement and refine your plan for balance. Much like how Gilbert set off on her journey in "Eat Pray Love", armed with resolve and anticipation, you too embark on your adventure, eager to shape your digital habits to serve your inner growth.

Begin by implementing your blueprint slowly. Do not rush. Attempting to change too many habits at once might be overwhelming. Start with one goal, perhaps the one that seems the most attainable or the one that aligns most closely with your immediate personal development needs. Once you achieve this goal, it will fuel your confidence to tackle the others.

Keep in mind that Rome wasn't built in a day and neither will your mindful relationship with technology. Be patient with yourself. This is a journey, not a destination. Like the growing global interest in mindfulness practices, consider your journey as a continuous process of self-discovery and growth.

As you make progress, stay alert to your experiences and emotions. Notice how each change is affecting your mood, your relationships and your personal growth. Are you feeling less anxious? Do you have more free time to pursue a hobby or spend with your loved ones? Are you feeling more fulfilled and less overwhelmed?

Make refinements to your blueprint based on these experiences. Remember, the key is flexibility. If a certain strategy isn't working for you, replace it. If a new digital distraction emerges, adapt your blueprint to address it.

To keep you motivated and accountable, consider sharing your journey with a friend or a mentor. This shall not only give you a support system but also allow you to share your insights and learn from others' experiences. You could even join online communities centered around digital mindfulness, much like the ashram Gilbert joined in India to deepen her spiritual understanding.

Lastly, don't forget to celebrate your progress. Even the smallest change—a reduced hour of screen time, a day without checking social media, an evening spent fully present with loved ones—marks a significant step in your journey towards digital mindfulness.

In this digital era, balance is not a luxury; it's a necessity. And this process of implementing and refining your blueprint is your journey towards creating that balance, towards finding your bliss in chaotic bytes.

Conclusion and Action steps

In this chapter, we've journeyed together through the bustling lanes of our digital lives, pausing to reflect, identify, strategize and implement. Just like Elizabeth Gilbert in "Eat Pray Love," we've taken a bold step towards self-discovery and personal development, amidst the clamor of our byte-driven world.

We started by assessing our current relationship with technology, reflecting upon our digital habits and acknowledging their impact on our lives. We then identified areas for growth, highlighting digital activities that serve us and those that detract from our personal development.

Drawing inspiration from the global trend towards mindfulness, we designed a personal blueprint for mindful living, weaving a vision of balance and setting tangible goals to realize this vision. And, finally, we set about implementing this blueprint, refining it based on our experiences, and celebrating each stride towards digital mindfulness.

As you close this chapter, remember that the journey doesn't end here. Like the practice of mindfulness, the pursuit of digital balance is a continuous process, a daily commitment to live intentionally, throughout the pull of technology.

Now, to ensure that you stay on the path of mindful tech usage, here are five action steps to guide you:

Reflect Daily: Take a few moments each day to assess your digital habits. This daily introspection will keep you attuned to your progress and aware of emerging distractions.

Set Boundaries: Establish tech-free zones or periods in your day. This could be meal times, the hour before bed or weekends. These tech-free intervals will reinforce your commitment to digital balance.

Use Tech Mindfully: Engage with technology intentionally. Be mindful of the content you consume and share online. Let your digital engagements enhance your personal growth, not detract from it.

Practice Digital Detox: Regularly disconnect from technology to reconnect with yourself and your surroundings. These moments of disconnection will serve as a reminder of the bliss that lies beyond bytes.

Celebrate Progress: Recognize and celebrate each small victory. Remember, every step, no matter how small, is a step towards a more mindful, balanced digital life.

Embrace these steps, just as you've embraced the journey thus far. Embark on the path to bytes and bliss with courage and conviction, always remembering that the ultimate goal is not to shun technology, but to use it in a way that enriches your journey towards personal development. And so, the journey continues...

Chapter 12

Embracing the Journey: A Lifetime of Bytes and Bliss

Just like the feather in the iconic opening scene of "Forrest Gump," our lives in the digital age seem to be carried along by an unseen wind. The story of Forrest, a man with an unwavering belief in the goodness of people and the power of love, might seem far removed from our fast-paced, technology-driven lives. Yet, at its core, this heartwarming narrative provides us with timeless lessons that are more relevant than ever.

As we navigate the endless tides of technological evolution, much like how Forrest navigates the trials and triumphs of his life, we too experience a myriad of emotions, challenges and victories. The characters in Forrest's life, the people he meets, and the situations he stumbles upon all create a beautiful tapestry that mirrors our journey in the digital age. With every byte of information we encounter, with every digital challenge we face, we get one step closer to finding our own bliss, our inner peace and our purpose.

In this chapter, we will uncover how to embrace this ongoing journey, just as Forrest embraced his. We will dive deep into accepting the ever-changing nature of technology, learn to adapt and evolve in a digital world, celebrate our successes and draw lessons from our setbacks. In doing so, we will foster a lifelong commitment to mindfulness and personal growth. This is not just a journey towards mastering the digital world but also towards reclaiming our true selves and finding bliss amidst the bytes.

Section 1: Accepting the ever-changing nature of technology

Section 2: Continuing to adapt and evolve in a digital world

Section 3: Celebrating successes and learning from setbacks

Section 4: Fostering a lifelong commitment to mindfulness and personal growth

Just as Forrest Gump accepted the flow of life, we too can harness the winds of technology, allowing them to guide us rather than control us. Let's embark on this transformative journey towards bytes and bliss. It is time for us to run towards our destiny, much like how Forrest ran towards his.

Section 1: Accepting the ever-changing nature of technology

Life is like a box of chocolates, as Forrest's mother famously said, you never know what you're going to get. It's a sentiment that rings true for our relationship with technology. We never know what the next update, the next app, the next device will bring into our lives. But just like Forrest, who accepted each chocolate, each life event, with grace and curiosity, we too can embrace the ever-changing nature of technology.

Accepting the fluid nature of technology doesn't mean we lose ourselves in it; instead, it means recognizing its transformative power and potential, much like Forrest recognized the potential in each character he met, no matter how brief their encounter. Whether it was Lieutenant Dan, who first appeared as a hardened soldier, or Jenny, whose journey was as tumultuous as it was heart-rending, Forrest saw the potential for change and growth in them. Similarly, each technological advancement brings with it the potential for personal growth, for discovering new ways to express ourselves, to connect and to learn.

In the digital age, change is the only constant. Technology evolves at a dizzying pace. Accepting this fact doesn't mean blindly adopting every new trend. Instead, it requires discernment. Just as Forrest chose which advice to take to heart and which to let go, we too must learn to choose which digital changes to incorporate into our lives and which to pass over.

Accepting the ever-changing nature of technology also requires a certain level of resilience. Just as Forrest braved storms, heartbreak and loss, we too must brave the disruptions that technology often brings. There will be moments when we feel overwhelmed, lost in the sea of information and updates, but these moments too shall pass. They are part of our journey, our story, our way to bytes and bliss.

Above all, acceptance requires an open heart and an open mind. Just like how Forrest embraced all that life threw at him with a guileless smile and a courageous heart, we too can embrace the fluctuations of the digital world. We must remember that every byte of information, every digital encounter, has the potential to bring us one step closer to our bliss, to our inner peace and to our life purpose.

It's time for us to accept the ever-changing nature of technology, not with fear or trepidation, but with the same courage, curiosity and grace that Forrest showed us. It's time to open our box of chocolates and embrace the surprises it holds.

Section 2: Continuing to Adapt and Evolve in a Digital World

Throughout his life, Forrest Gump showed us the power of adaptation. Despite the odds, whether it was being fitted with leg braces as a child, being drafted into the army, or losing his beloved Jenny, Forrest always found a way to adapt and keep moving forward. In a similar vein, as we navigate through our digital journey, we must also learn to adapt and evolve with the changing tides of technology.

Consider the evolution of communication over the years, from snail mail to email, from landlines to smartphones and from face-to-face conversations to video calls. Each change required us to adapt and relearn. And while these transitions can often feel daunting, it's important to remember that with each shift, we have also expanded our capabilities, enhanced our ability to connect and discovered new means of expression.

As we step into the world of tweets, likes, shares and instant messages, our social interaction's face changes, much like the changing faces in Forrest's life. Like the chameleon, we too must adapt to these changes. Yet, it's equally essential to stay true to ourselves amidst this digital transformation, much like Forrest remained his authentic self despite his circumstances.

Embrace technology as a tool, a means to an end, and not an end in itself. As we learn to use these tools, let us not forget the core of our being, our essential humanity. Because while technology can provide us with countless conveniences and opportunities, it is our values, our compassion and our respect for one another that define us.

Adapting and evolving in a digital world also means continually learning. Just as Forrest learned to play ping-pong, to run a shrimping boat, to care for his son, we too can learn to navigate the digital world with grace and efficiency. This constant learning and unlearning are integral to our digital journey and to our pursuit of bytes and bliss.

Just as Forrest showed us that life does not stop for anyone, so too does technology. It is continuously evolving, constantly in flux. And as we continue to adapt and evolve with it, we begin to see that this journey is not just about surviving in a digital world. It's about thriving in it. It's about finding our bliss amidst the bytes.

Section 3: Celebrating Successes and Learning from Setbacks

In Forrest Gump's life, we saw a mix of triumphs and trials, joys and sorrows, successes and setbacks. Yet, through it all, Forrest maintained a humble and optimistic outlook on life. He celebrated his successes without arrogance, learned from his setbacks without self-pity and found joy in the simplest of things. As we journey through the digital landscape, there's a profound lesson to be learned from Forrest's approach.

Consider the joy that Forrest derived from his successes, be it his All-American football achievement, his ping-pong championship or his successful shrimping business. He savored these victories without arrogance, never letting them overshadow his naivety and kindness. Similarly, as we navigate through our digital world, we too will encounter successes. Perhaps you've mastered a new software, built an impressive online following or created a digital product that people love. These are victories to be celebrated, moments to be enjoyed. Yet, just as Forrest did, we must also remember to stay grounded and humble, to appreciate the journey that led us to these victories.

Forrest also encountered numerous setbacks throughout his life, yet he faced them with a heart full of hope and a spirit that refused to be broken. Whether it meant being separated from his mother, losing his best friend Bubba or facing the heartbreaking loss of Jenny, Forrest took these challenges in stride. He learned from them, grew from them and moved forward with an unbroken spirit.

Likewise, in our digital journey, we too shall face setbacks. There will be times when technology frustrates us, when we fail to understand a new concept, or when a project we've worked on falls apart. But these setbacks are not roadblocks; they are stepping stones. They are opportunities to learn, to grow and become stronger. Just as Forrest did, we too must learn to see the silver lining in our digital clouds.

Our journey in the digital world, much like Forrest's journey through life, shall be filled with ups and downs, triumphs and trials, successes, and setbacks. But with each victory we shall celebrate and with each setback we shall learn and grow. Because at the end of the day, it's not just about the destination; it's about the journey.

Section 4: Fostering a Lifelong Commitment to Mindfulness and Personal Growth

From start to finish, the story of Forrest Gump is a testament to personal growth and resilience. Despite the hurdles he encountered and the people who doubted him, Forrest never stopped growing, never stopped moving forward. His journey, both inspiring and touching, offers us invaluable insights into how we can foster a lifelong commitment to mindfulness and personal growth amidst our digital lives.

In this digital era, we are constantly bombarded with information, much like the array of experiences that Forrest encountered in his life. Yet, amidst this barrage of bytes, Forrest's approach teaches us the power of mindfulness—of being present and focused. He taught us to listen attentively, whether to his mother's wisdom, Bubba's shrimping techniques or Jenny's love. This ability to be present, to listen and absorb, is a powerful tool in navigating our digital lives. It allows us to sift through the noise, to focus on what truly matters and to be fully present in our interactions, both online and offline.

Mindfulness in our digital journey also means being aware of how technology affects us—how it influences our emotions, our behaviors and our relationships. It's about recognizing when technology enhances our lives and when it drains our energy. This awareness empowers us to make mindful choices about how we use technology and how we allow it to shape our lives.

Just as Forrest committed to growing and learning throughout his life, we too need to foster a commitment to personal growth in our digital journey. It's about constantly learning, adapting and evolving with the changing digital landscape. It's about being open to new experiences, new knowledge and new opportunities for growth.

But most importantly, this journey towards personal growth is also a journey inwards. It's about connecting with our authentic selves amidst the digital noise. It's about uncovering our inner strengths, our passions and our purpose, much like Forrest discovered his love for running, his knack for ping-pong and his capacity for unconditional love.

Fostering a lifelong commitment to mindfulness and personal growth in our digital lives is a continuous transformation—a journey of learning, of growing and of becoming the best versions of ourselves. As we step into the bytes of information and the waves of digital distractions, let's also step into the bliss of personal growth and mindfulness.

Conclusion and Action Steps

Just like the powerful narrative of Forrest Gump, our journey in the digital world is filled with ups and downs, victories and setbacks, learning and unlearning. We've explored the importance of accepting the ever-changing nature of technology, of adapting and evolving with it, of celebrating our successes, learning from our setbacks and fostering a lifelong commitment to mindfulness and personal growth. This journey, with its bytes and bliss, is both challenging and rewarding. But remember, just as Forrest kept running, we too must keep moving forward in our digital journey.

Action Steps:

Embrace the Change: Take some time each day to learn about new technological advancements. Understand how they can enhance your life and contribute to your personal growth.

Stay Grounded: While celebrating your digital victories, remember to stay humble. Appreciate the journey that led to those successes and remember the lessons learned along the way.

Learn from Setbacks: When faced with digital challenges, instead of giving up, take a moment to understand what went wrong. Use these setbacks as opportunities to learn and grow.

Practice Mindfulness: Regularly take breaks from your digital devices. Use this time to reconnect with yourself, with nature and with those around you. Remember, technology is a tool, not the master.

Commit to Personal Growth: Make a commitment to continually learn and grow in your digital journey. Be open to new experiences, new knowledge and new opportunities.

And so, dear friend, we invite you to embark on a journey that mirrors the very essence of Forrest Gump's voyage, weaving through the ever-evolving labyrinth of technology with elegance, modesty, tenacity and an unquenchable thirst for personal growth. Together, let's find our harmony amidst the digital symphony of bytes. And remember, just as Forrest's mother wisely said, "Life is like a box of chocolates. You never know what you're gonna get."

However, we assure you that no matter what you're served from life's assortment of experiences, you have within you the strength to navigate it, the potential to learn from it, and the ability to savor it. We celebrate your courage, your commitment and your curiosity that brought you here, walking this path of inner exploration amidst the whirlwind of the digital world.

Thank you for investing precious moments of your life in the pursuit of inner growth, for in doing so, you're contributing to a future that is brighter, kinder and more mindful. Please know that you are never alone in this journey. Each step you take towards your personal growth resonates with countless others walking this path, amplifying our collective quest for purpose, connection and true fulfillment in this digital age.

Let this book be your companion, your guide and your reminder that within the buzz and hum of the digital world, a blissful silence resides, a silence that echoes the song of your true self. It is there that you will find your bliss amidst the bytes. Your journey doesn't end here; rather, it takes a new leap into uncharted territories of self-discovery, empowerment and authentic living.

In this grand odyssey of life, may you always find the courage to keep exploring, the wisdom to embrace the rhythm of change and the joy of knowing that every step you take contributes to the beautiful dance of life. From one traveler to another, our journey together may end here, but your personal journey towards bytes and bliss has just begun. Godspeed my friend!